CAMBRIDGE

IELTS Trainer

Academic

Six Practice Tests

2

Cambridge University Press
www.cambridge.org/elt

Cambridge Assessment English
www.cambridgeenglish.org

Information on this title: www.cambridge.org/9781108567589

© Cambridge University Press and UCLES 2019

This publication is in copyright. Subject to statutory exception
and to the provisions of relevant collective licensing agreements,
no reproduction of any part may take place without the written
permission of Cambridge University Press.

First published 2019

20 19 18 17 16 15 14 13 12 11 10 9 8 7 6 5 4 3 2 1

Printed in Malaysia by Vivar Printing

A catalogue record for this publication is available from the British Library

ISBN 978-1-108-56758-9 Academic Student's Book with Resources Download
ISBN 978-1-108-59366-3 General Training Student's Book with Resources Download

Cambridge University Press has no responsibility for the persistence or accuracy
of URLs for external or third-party internet websites referred to in this publication,
and does not guarantee that any content on such websites is, or will remain,
accurate or appropriate. Information regarding prices, travel timetables, and other
factual information given in this work is correct at the time of first printing but
Cambridge University Press does not guarantee the accuracy of such information thereafter.

It is normally necessary for written permission for copying to be obtained
in advance from a publisher. The answer sheets at the back of this book are designed to be copied
and distributed in class.

The normal requirements are waived here and it is not necessary to write to
Cambridge University Press for permission for an individual teacher to make copies
for use within his or her own classroom. Only those pages that carry the wording
'© UCLES 2019 Photocopiable Photocopiable ' may be copied.

Contents

Introduction		4

Training and Exam Practice

Test 1	Listening	10
	Reading	23
	Writing	43
	Speaking	58
Test 2	Listening	64
	Reading	75
	Writing	91
	Speaking	99

Practice Tests

Test 3	Listening	105
	Reading	111
	Writing	122
	Speaking	123
Test 4	Listening	124
	Reading	130
	Writing	141
	Speaking	142
Test 5	Listening	143
	Reading	149
	Writing	160
	Speaking	161
Test 6	Listening	162
	Reading	168
	Writing	178
	Speaking	179

Sample Answer Sheets		180
Acknowledgements		184

Introduction

What is IELTS?

The International English Language Testing System (IELTS) is widely recognised as a test of the language ability of candidates who need to study or work where English is the language of communication.

There are two types of IELTS test: the Academic Module (taken for entry to undergraduate or postgraduate studies or for professional reasons) and the General Training Module (taken for entry to vocational or training programmes not at degree level and for immigration purposes). Both modules are made up of four tests – Listening, Reading, Writing and Speaking. The Listening and Speaking tests are the same for both Academic and General Training but the Reading and Writing tests are different.

Who is *IELTS Trainer Academic* for?

This book is suitable for anyone who is preparing to take the IELTS Academic Module. *IELTS Trainer* can be used in class with a teacher or by students working on their own at home. It is aimed at candidates who would like to achieve a Band Score of 6 or higher. (See section on Scoring on page 6.)

What is *IELTS Trainer Academic*?

This book contains six practice tests for IELTS, each covering the Listening, Reading, Writing and Speaking papers. The practice tests in Guided Tests 1 and 2 are also accompanied by training and advice. All six tests are at the level of the exam.

In Test 1 each part of each paper consists of a training section and an exam practice section:

- The training sections have information and exercises to help you prepare for each part of the paper. In the Listening, Writing and Speaking papers, Test 1 presents and practises grammar, vocabulary and functional language relevant to those papers. This is supported by work on correcting common errors made by IELTS candidates in the exam, as shown by the **Cambridge Learner Corpus** (see page 6). In Writing, there are extracts from the scripts of IELTS candidates as well as sample answers.

- The exam practice sections consist of the test itself accompanied by step-by-step guidance for each task, with tips on strategy and advice linked to the questions. There is a wide range of tasks in the IELTS Listening and Reading papers and the same task may not always appear in the same part of the exam every time. The practice tests reflect this variety and training is given in Tests 1 and 2 in all the major task types which you will come across.

Test 2 contains training for the exam focusing on the task types not covered in Test 1, in addition to a review of the information in Test 1. The training sections are shorter in Test 2 than in Test 1. Test 2 also contains an exam practice section with tips and advice on how to deal with the practice test itself.

Tests 3–6 are complete practice tests without advice or training. They contain variations of the task types in Tests 1 and 2 and cover a wide range of topics and text types. They give you the opportunity to practise the strategies and skills you have acquired while working through Tests 1 and 2.

There is an **Explanatory answer key** (see page 5) for each test available to download from esource.cambridge.org.

How to use IELTS Trainer Academic

Test 1 Training
- For each part of the paper (e.g. Listening Part 1, page 10), first read the overview **What is ...?**, describing the type(s) of task which that part may contain. For some parts there is also a section called **What does it test?** which describes, for example, the kind of skills that part of the exam tests (e.g. identifying key facts, understanding speakers' opinions).
- Read through the **Task information**, which describes in detail the particular task type that follows.
- Look at the information marked **Tip**, which gives general advice on exam strategy and language.
- Work through **Useful language** exercises in the Listening, Writing and Speaking sections before tackling the exam tasks on the practice pages. These training exercises help to develop the necessary skills and offer practice directly relevant to the exam tasks in Test 1. Answers to the exercises are in the **Explanatory answer key** (available to download from esource.cambridge.org). Many exercises involve focusing on and correcting common language mistakes made by actual IELTS candidates, as shown by the **Cambridge Learner Corpus** (see page 6).
- Check the boxes marked **Advice**. These give practical help with individual questions.
- In **Listening**, use the audio files available to download with the audioscripts from esource.cambridge.org.
- In Test 1 **Writing**, many exercises are based on language used in IELTS essays in the **Cambridge Learner Corpus** and sample answers written by actual IELTS candidates. There are also sample answers which show what is expected of the best candidates. The **Explanatory answer key** contains answers to the exercises. These training exercises build up to an exam task at the end which is similar to, but not the same as, those in the training exercises.
- In **Speaking**, there are exercises which build into a bank of personalised, useful language for the first part of the test and other exercises which practise the language necessary for the prepared talk and discussion which follow in Parts 2 and 3. These can be used with a partner, or when working alone, for timed practice.

Test 1 Exam Practice
- Read the **Action plan** for each task in the Listening, Reading and Writing papers immediately before working through the exam practice task. There are many different task types and the Action plans show how to approach each type in the best way to achieve good marks and avoid wasting time.
- Work through the task, carefully following the steps of the Action plan and making use of the help in the **Tip** information and **Advice** boxes.
- Answers to all items are in the **Explanatory answer key**, which explains why the correct answers are right and others are wrong.

Test 2 Training
- Answer the questions in the **Review** section to remind yourself about each part of the test. If you need to, look back at Test 1 to check your answers.
- Work through the exercises in the Writing and Speaking sections. The Speaking section extends the strategies and skills introduced in Test 1 and adds to the topics which you might be asked about. The Writing section revises the strategies covered in Test 1 and offers further targeted language training exercises. Many of the exercises are based on IELTS candidates' answers from the **Cambridge Learner Corpus**.

Test 2 Exam Practice
- Answer the questions in each **Action plan reminder**. These ask you about strategies which were introduced in Test 1. Use the cross-reference to refer back to Test 1 if you need to.
- Read through the **Action plans** for the new task types which weren't in Test 1. Use the **Tip** information and **Advice** boxes to help you do the tasks and the **Explanatory answer key** to check your answers.

Tests 3–6 Exam Practice
- Try to do the exam tasks under exam conditions where possible, applying the skills and language learnt in Training Tests 1 and 2.

- For the Speaking paper, it is better to work with a partner so that you can ask each other the questions. If that is not possible, follow the instructions and do all three parts alone. Use a watch and keep to the correct time. Recording the test and listening to it can help you identify language areas which need more practice.

You can do Tests 3–6 in any order, but you should always try to keep to the time recommended for each paper.

The Cambridge Learner Corpus

The Cambridge Learner Corpus (CLC) is a large collection of exam scripts written by students taking Cambridge Assessment English exams around the world. It currently contains over over 55 million words and is growing all the time. It forms part of the Cambridge English Corpus and it has been built up by Cambridge University Press and Cambridge Assessment English. The CLC currently contains scripts from over:

- over 220,000 students
- 173 different first languages
- 200 different countries

Exercises and extracts from candidates' answers from Writing in *IELTS Trainer Academic* which are based on the CLC are indicated by this icon:

Other components of *IELTS Trainer Academic*

- The **Explanatory answer key** gives the correct answers, and explains them where necessary (especially in Tests 1 and 2). In some cases, such as multiple-choice questions, it also explains why the other possible answers are wrong.
- The full **Transcripts** for the Listening papers are available to download from esource.cambridge.org
- **Answer sheets** for the Listening, Reading and Writing papers are at the back of the book. Before you take the exam, you should study these so that you know how to mark or write your answers correctly.
- **Audio** recordings for the Listening papers are available to download from esource.cambridge.org. The listening material is indicated by an icon in *IELTS Trainer Academic*:

International English Language Testing System (IELTS)

Level of IELTS

You do not pass or fail IELTS. You get a Band Score between 1 and 9. Candidates scoring 9 have fluent, accurate English, with wide-ranging vocabulary. They make very few errors and will be capable of performing in English in professional and academic contexts. Candidates scoring 7 can understand and communicate effectively in English, using some complex language, and although there may be errors, these do not impede communication. A score of 5 or lower means that the candidate has a limited range of language and that errors in grammar, pronunciation, etc. lead to misunderstandings.

Different organisations and institutions publish the Band Score they require for entry.

Scoring

The Listening test contains 40 items and each correct item is given one mark.

The Reading test contains 40 items and each correct item is given one mark. The Academic and General Training Reading Tests are graded to the same level. However, because the texts in the Academic Reading Test are more challenging overall than those in the General Training Test, more questions need to be answered correctly on a General Training Test to receive the same grade.

The Writing test (both Academic and General Training) is marked on the following areas: Task Achievement (for Task 1), Task Response (for Task 2), Coherence and Cohesion, Lexical Resource, Grammatical Range and Accuracy. Examiners give a Band Score for each of these criteria, which are equally weighted.

For the Speaking test, a Band Score is given for each of the following, which are equally weighted: Fluency and Coherence, Lexical Resource, Grammatical Range and Pronunciation.

Candidates receive scores on a Band Scale from 1 to 9 for each skill tested (Listening, Reading, Writing and Speaking). They are of equal importance. These four scores are then averaged and rounded to produce an Overall Band Score. Each candidate receives a Test Report Form setting out their Overall Band Score and their scores for each test. The scores are reported in whole bands or half bands according to the nine-band score given below.

If you do the practice tests in *IELTS Trainer Academic* under exam conditions, you need to score approximately 20 marks on both the Reading and Listening tests for a Band Score of around 5.5. To achieve a Band Score of 7, you need approximately 30 marks in both Reading and Listening.

IELTS Band Scores

9 Expert user – Has fully operational command of the language: appropriate, accurate and fluent with complete understanding.

8 Very good user – Has fully operational command of the language with only occasional unsystematic inaccuracies and inappropriacies. Misunderstandings may occur in unfamiliar situations. Handles complex, detailed argumentation well.

7 Good user – Has operational command of the language, though with occasional inaccuracies, inappropriacies and misunderstandings in some situations. Generally handles complex language well and understands detailed reasoning.

6 Competent user – Has generally effective command of the language despite some inaccuracies, inappropriacies and misunderstandings. Can use and understand fairly complex language, particularly in familiar situations.

5 Modest user – Has partial command of the language, coping with overall meaning in most situations, though is likely to make many mistakes. Should be able to handle basic communication in own field.

4 Limited user – Basic competence is limited to familiar situations. Has frequent problems in understanding and expression. Is not able to use complex language.

3 Extremely limited user – Conveys and understands only general meaning in very familiar situations. Frequent breakdowns in communication occur.

2 Intermittent user – No real communication is possible except for the most basic information using isolated words or short formulae in familiar situations and to meet immediate needs. Has great difficulty understanding spoken and written English.

1 Non-user – Essentially has no ability to use the language beyond possibly a few isolated words.

0 Did not attempt the test – No assessable information provided.

For more information on grading and results, go to the Cambridge Assessment English website (see page 9).

Content of IELTS

IELTS has four papers, each consisting of two, three or four parts. For details on each paper, see below.

Paper 1 Listening about 30 minutes, with 10 minutes at the end to transfer answers to the answer sheet

- This paper is common to both the Academic and General Training Modules.
- The topics in Parts 1 and 2 are based around social situations but the topics in Parts 3 and 4 are all in an educational or training context.
- The **level of difficulty** increases from Part 1 to Part 4.
- Each part is heard **once only**.
- The **instructions** for each task are on the question paper.
- There is a short **pause** before each part which can be used to look at the task and questions. Where there is more than one task in a part, there is also a short pause before the part of the recording which relates to the next task.
- A brief introductory explanation of the **context** is heard before each part, but is **not** printed on the question paper.
- Correct **spelling** is essential on the answer sheet.

Paper 1 Listening

Part	No. of questions	Text type	Task types *Each part has one or more of these task types*	Task information
1	10	a conversation or interview between two speakers, giving and exchanging information about an everyday topic	table, note and form completion	page 10
2	10	a monologue (sometimes introduced by another speaker) giving information on an everyday topic, e.g. a radio programme or talk from a guide	plan / map labelling multiple-choice flow-chart completion sentence completion matching tasks	pages 14 pages 14, 17 page 17 page 20 page 67
3	10	a conversation between two, three or four speakers in an educational or training context		
4	10	a monologue in an academic setting, e.g. a lecture or presentation		

Paper 2 Academic Reading 1 hour

- This paper is only taken in the Academic Module. There is a different paper for candidates taking the General Training Module (see Cambridge Assessment English website). Both papers follow the same format but the kinds of texts on the two modules differ in terms of topic, genre, complexity of language and style.
- There are approximately 2,750 words in total in the three passages.

Passage	No. of questions	Text types	Task types *Each passage has one or more of these task types*	Task information
1	13 (two or three tasks)	Texts may be from books, journals, magazines, newspapers or websites. They are suitable for reading by undergraduate or postgraduate students but are of general interest, not only for subject specialists.	true / false / not given	page 23
2	13 (three tasks)		table, note, flow-chart completion, diagram labelling	page 24
3	14 (three tasks)		matching headings	page 29
			matching sentences with people	page 29
			summary completion	page 30
			multiple-choice	pages 36, 83
			matching sentence endings	page 37
			matching information	page 80
			sentence completion	page 82
			yes / no / not given	page 89

8 | Introduction

Paper 3 Academic Writing 1 hour

This paper is only taken in the Academic Module. There is a different paper for candidates taking the General Training Module (see Cambridge Assessment English website).

Task	Suggested time and marks	Task text type and number of words	Task information and practice
1	20 minutes one-third of the marks for the paper	a summary of information given in a graph, chart, table or diagram 150 words minimum	pages 43–50
2	40 minutes two-thirds of the marks for the paper	a discussion essay in response to a statement of opinion or ideas 250 words minimum	pages 51–57

Paper 4 Speaking 11–14 minutes

This paper is common to both the Academic and General Training Modules.

It is a face-to-face interview with an examiner and is recorded.

Part	Time	Task type	Task information and practice
1	4–5 minutes	giving personal information and discussing everyday subjects	pages 58–59
2	1 minute preparation 2 minutes talk	giving a prepared talk on a subject given by the examiner and answering one or two follow-up questions	pages 60–61
3	4–5 minutes	a discussion with the examiner arising from the topic of Part 2, offering the opportunity to discuss more abstract issues and ideas	page 62

Further information

The information about IELTS contained in *IELTS Trainer Academic* is designed to be an overview of the exam. For a full description of IELTS, including information about task types, testing focus and preparation for the exam, please see the *IELTS Handbook*, which can be obtained from Cambridge Assessment English at the address below or from the website at:

www.cambridgeenglish.org

Cambridge Assessment English

The Triangle Building

Shaftesbury Road

Cambridge CB2 8EA

United Kingdom

Training Test 1 — Listening Part 1

What is Listening Part 1?
- a conversation between two people, either face to face or on the phone
- one or two tasks (e.g. table completion)
- an example and 10 questions

The purpose of the conversation is to communicate and share information that will be useful in some way (e.g. for making a holiday booking, for working out the best transport options).

What does it test?
- understanding specific information e.g. dates, prices, everyday objects, locations
- spelling of people and place names

Task information: *Table, Note and Form completion*

This task requires you to fill in the spaces in the table. The spaces are numbered in the same order as the information you hear.

You have to:
- listen to a conversation, which you hear once only.
- write one to three words, a number, or a date in each space in the table.
- write the exact words you hear.
- spell everything correctly.

Useful language: spelling

In Part 1, a speaker will sometimes spell out the name of a person, street or company.

You need to be very familiar with the English names for the letters of the alphabet, as the word will only be spelt out once.

01   **1**   Listen and choose the first letter in each pair that you hear.

1 A/E	2 A/I	3 E/I	4 A/R
5 Y/E	6 O/U	7 B/P	8 G/J
9 S/F	10 M/N	11 H/X	12 D/T

02   **2**   Listen to some words being spelt out and write down what you hear.

1 Manager: Sarah ....
2 Email: .... @gmail.com
3 Meeting point: .... School sports field
4 Hotel name: ....
5 Address: 112 .... Terrace
6 Company: .... Movers

Advice
Not all place names are spelt out. For example, the underlined words are very common in English, so you should learn how to spell words like these.

<u>Mountain</u> View Hotel
<u>Ocean</u> Road
<u>Bridge</u> Street

Advice
When we say a phone number, we can pronounce 0 as **oh**, or say **zero**.

When we talk about money we say, for example, **seven pounds / dollars / euros fifty**. (£7.50, $7.50, €7.50).

Useful language: numbers

03   **1**   Listen and write the numbers you hear.

1 Customer cell phone: ....
2 Distance of race: .... miles
3 A one-way ticket is: ....
4 Home address: .... Bayside Road.
5 Width of window frame: .... inches
6 Booking reference: ....

TIP
The answer can be written in numerals or in letters, e.g. 650, or six hundred and fifty. But it's much easier and faster to write numerals!

TIP
For similar sounding numbers, listen out for the stressed syllable e.g. fif<u>teen</u>, <u>fif</u>ty, six<u>teen</u>, <u>six</u>ty.

Useful language: times and dates

🎧 **1 Listen and write the times or dates you hear.**
04
1 Arrival date: ....
2 Class schedule: .... to 6:30 p.m.
3 Date of last inspection: ...., 2018
4 Best time to visit: ....
5 The courses finishes on: ....
6 Delivery date: ....

> **Advice**
>
> We say dates like *1752* or *1997* as **seventeen fifty-two** and **nineteen ninety-seven**. For years following 2000, we can say, for example, **two thousand eighteen**, or **two thousand and /ən/ eighteen**, or **twenty eighteen**.

Useful language: recognising when the answer is coming

In Part 1, you might see a question like 'Height: about **1** ....cm'.
You might not hear the word 'height' in the recording. Instead, the speaker might ask a question, or say something that relates to a person's height. This will tell you when the answer is coming.

> **TIP** You can write a date in different ways to get a mark (e.g. 3rd March, March 3 or 3 March). This fits the **one word and / or a number** in the instruction.

1 Match an answer 1-6 with a question A-F the speaker might ask.

Height: around **1** ...*6*...... feet	A 'So can you tell me how long the curtains are?'
Width: **2** ...*15*...... centimetres	B 'How tall are the trees at the moment – approximately?'
Distance: **3** ...*26*...... kilometres	C 'And what would the charge for that be?'
Length: **4** ...*330*...... inches	D 'How heavy is the box you want us to move?'
Weight: about **5** ...*63*...... kg	E 'Do you know how wide the screen is?'
Cost: **6** $ ...*560*...	F 'How far is it from the hotel to the airport?'

> **TIP** Don't add words like **euros** or **inches** or **kilometres** to the answer sheet if they are provided on the question paper.

Useful strategy: deciding what to write in the spaces

1 Look at the sample exam task below and complete this table.

Which space needs ...		What tells you this?
a date?	8	the verb 'starts' and 'Wednesday'.
a price?		
a phone number?		
a person's name		
a period of time?		
a place?		
a piece of equipment or clothing – singular noun?		
a piece of equipment or clothing – plural noun?		
a verb / action?		
a part of the body?		

TIP Predicting what type of word will go into each space helps you to be ready to hear it during the recording.

Advice
*Speakers sometimes mention a time, date or number, which might fit a space, but is not the real answer. This is called a **distraction**. Listen carefully in case the speaker changes their mind, or another speaker corrects them with the real time, date or number.*

Westwood Community Centre Activities

Classes: when / where
Yoga basics
Example:
Mondays 7 p.m. – *8:30* p.m.
Taking place in the hall

Things to bring
a **1** .... is necessary for every session

Other information
Discounted rate for students:
2 $ ....

Simple techniques that will help you
3 .... pain in your **4** ....

Classes: when / where
Westwood Walkers
7:00 a.m. every morning

The walk starts from outside the
5 .... in the village

Things to bring
A good pair of
6 .... will help

Other information
Free for everyone

The organiser is **7** ....
Lindsay

Classes: when / where
Cycle Group
Training starts again on
Wednesday, **8** ....

The rides take about
9 .... on average

Things to bring
helmet and bike lights are essential

Other information
No charge

Nicky's contact details:
10 ....

12 Training Test 1   Listening Part 1

Exam Practice Test 1 — Listening Part 1

Action plan for *Table completion*
1. Look at the instructions to find out how many words you can write.
2. Look at the heading and the subheadings. There is time to do this before you listen.
3. Look at the spaces and think about what kinds of word or number are needed (e.g. a date, a distance, an address, a plural noun).
4. Listen to the introduction, which tells you what the conversation is about.
5. Listen carefully to the conversation and focus on each question in turn. As soon as you've written the answer to one question, listen for the answer to the next.
6. Move on to the next row each time the speaker talks about something new – in this case, a new class.

TIP Write an answer in each space even if you aren't sure about it. A guess might turn out to be right and get a mark, but an empty space won't be given a mark.

TIP The question numbers run horizontally across each row.

TIP If one of your answers is more than one word and a number, it is wrong, and won't get a mark.

TIP Remember you only hear the recording once.

Questions 1–10
Complete the table below.
Write **ONE WORD AND / OR A NUMBER** for each answer.

Art classes at Bramley Community Centre

Class	Things to bring	Fees / Timetable	Tutor
Example 'Movement and ..*light*..': painting in the style of French Impressionists	a set of **1** .... is essential	The cost is **2** $ .... for two terms Monday evenings 6–8 p.m., Room 15	A local artist called Steve **3** ....
'Clay basics': using the pottery wheel to make several **4**	an old **5** .... would be a good idea	The cost is $180 per term Every **6** .... 6:30–8:30 p.m., Room 3	Theresa Clark – her work is displayed in the community centre
'Sketching Architecture': drawing old buildings, starting with the **7**	people usually take a fold-up chair and a **8**	The cost is $160 per term Fridays 11–1 p.m. meet at the corner of Victoria Street and **9** .... Road	Annie Li Annie's cell phone number: **10** ....

Advice
1 Should the noun you write be plural or singular?
2 Make sure the answer you choose is for two terms, not one.
4 Use your general knowledge to predict the kind of things people might make in a pottery class. And note the word **several**.
5 Listen for the word **old**, a similar adjective, or a paraphrase in the recording. This may signal that the answer is coming soon. Note that the occurrence of the same adjective (old) in both the recording and the question is unusual.
6 What does the word **every** tell you about the kind of noun that is needed?
7 The answer must be a kind of building. Listen carefully – because one or more buildings might be mentioned as distraction.

Training Test 1 — Listening Part 2

What is Listening Part 2?
- a talk / speech / announcement / recorded message / radio excerpt given by one person, sometimes with an introduction by another person
- usually two tasks (e.g. multiple-choice, matching, flow-chart completion, plan / map labelling)
- 10 questions; there is a brief pause in the recording before the start of the next task

Task information: *Plan / map labelling*

Plan / map labelling requires you to transfer the information you hear to a simple plan / map. You need to follow language expressing where things are located.

You have to:
- listen to part of the talk, which you hear once only.
- match a list of places to their locations (labelled A, B, C etc.) on the plan / map.
- write A, B, C etc. next to the corresponding place in the list.

The speaker's purpose is to provide information that will be useful in some way (e.g. to inform staff about new health and safety requirements, to give directions to a group of volunteers, to tell people about a local event they could attend).

What does it test?
- identifying specific factual information and detail
- understanding stated opinion

Task information: *5-option multiple-choice*

Multiple-choice questions usually focus on the details. The questions follow the order of the recording, although the options A–E do not.

You have to:
- listen to the recording, which you'll hear only once.
- choose two options from a list of five, i.e. A–E.

There is another kind of multiple-choice task – see Test 1 Part 3.

Useful language: *plan / map labelling* tasks

For Part 2, you will need to recognise language for directions.

1 Look at the places marked on the plan. Complete the sentences with phrases from the box. (Usually there are not so many labelled buildings on the map, or complete sentences.)

| at the top | directly below | in between | in the centre | just above | nearest to |
| right-hand corner | smaller of | square-shaped | surrounded by | the south | to the right |

PLAN OF UNIVERSITY CAMPUS

1 As you can see, Student Services is at the bottom of your plan. .... of Student Services is a row of three lecture halls. The Albert Lecture Hall is the one ....
2 The Arts Block is .... the Science Block, and .... the Student Services building.
3 See the two L-shaped buildings at the top of the plan, in the ....? The Main Library is the .... those two buildings.
4 The Sports Complex is easy to find. See the circular running track .... of the map? On the left of that are two long, rectangular buildings. The Sports Complex is the one .... the running track.
5 The café is well situated on the campus. .... the science block and the car park – there's a .... building complex where many seminars take place. And in the centre of that building complex, you can find the café.
6 The nursery is in a nice spot. It's that building to .... of the car park. The one that's .... trees.

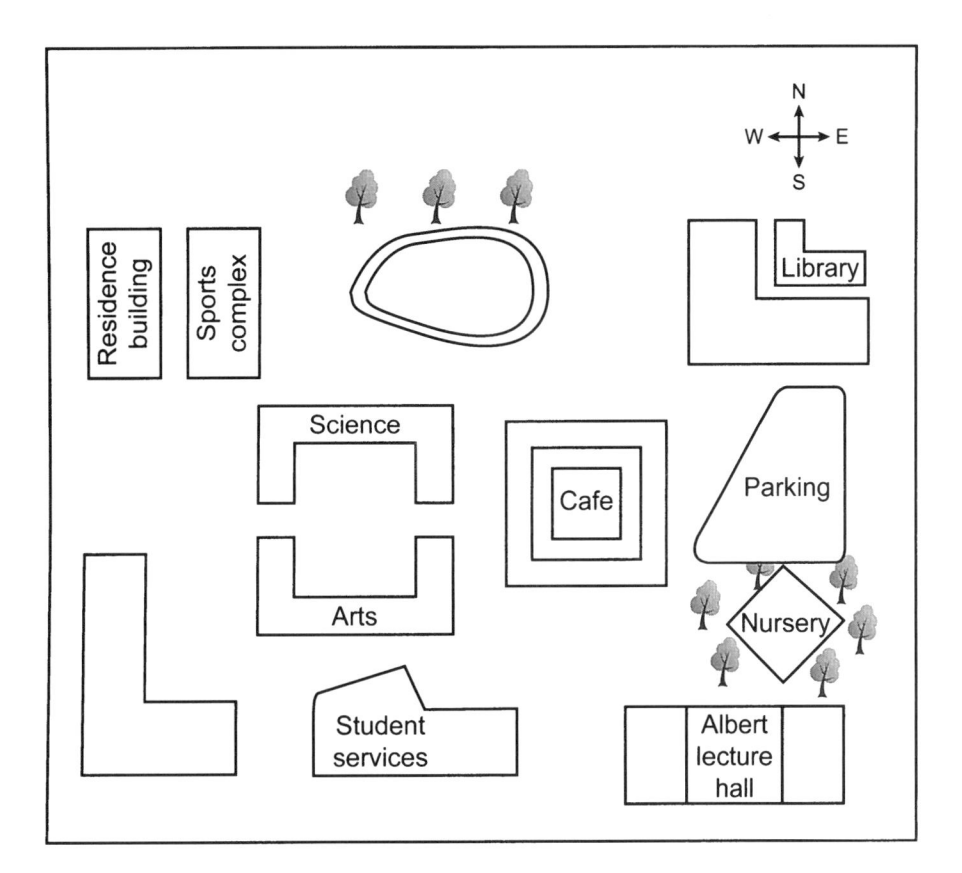

2 Listen and check your answers.

Useful strategy: paraphrasing in *5-option multiple-choice* tasks

In many IELTS tasks, you have to choose a correct answer from a number of options. The options may use different language to express ideas mentioned in the recording. This is known as 'paraphrasing'.

1   Match options A–E with extracts 1–5.

   Underline the parts of the extracts that match the underlined phrases in the options.

   A   dealing with unhappy clients on the phone
   B   improving written communication skills
   C   giving presentations to colleagues
   D   filing documents correctly
   E   being a mentor to junior members of staff

   1   So one thing the session will cover is how to deal with the huge amount of paperwork we receive. In other words, how we organise and store it all, in the right way, I mean.
   2   I've been impressed by the way you've all managed to stand up and deliver a talk to the other people on your team. I don't think we need any more training in that area for now.
   3   When a dissatisfied customer rings you up to complain, you need to know how to handle the situation effectively. We dealt with this in the previous session.
   4   As you know, we have a number of trainees starting work next week. We don't have time to talk about this in the training session, but I'd like you to support and guide them during their first few months in the company.
   5   From time to time you need to produce formal reports and the aim of this training session is to show you how to express your ideas more effectively and clearly.

Exam Practice Test 1 — Listening Part 2

Action plan for *5-option multiple-choice*
1. Read the questions so you know what kind of information you need to listen for.
2. Underline key words and ideas in the options and remember these may be paraphrased in the recording.
3. Listen to the introduction. It tells you who is speaking and describes the situation.
4. Transfer your answers to the answer sheet at the end of the test.

TIP You can write the two options in any order on the answer sheet (e.g. A / B or B / A)

Questions 11–12
Choose TWO letters, A–E.

Which **TWO** things will employees need to do during their first week in their new office space?

A find out about safety procedures
B collect a new form of identification
C move boxes containing documents
D make a note of any problem that occurs
E learn about new company technology

Advice
11–12 Listen out for ideas which might be paraphrased in the options. Make sure the options you choose match exactly what the speaker says.
13–14 The options may not be in the same order as in the recording. Cross them off when you think they have been paraphrased.

Questions 13–14
Choose TWO letters, A–E.

Which **TWO** steps have the company taken to improve the physical environment of employees' offices?

A provided comfortable seating
B installed a new heating system
C used attractive materials
D enlarged people's working space
E replaced the old type of lights

Action plan for *Plan / map labelling*
1. Read the instructions and the list of places you have to locate.
2. Quickly scan the plan for places, buildings or objects already labelled.
3. Identify any useful features that might be mentioned in the talk, e.g. a bridge, and look for arrows for north, south, etc.
4. As you listen, write the letters (**A**, **B**, **C**, etc.) next to the list of places.
5. Transfer your answers to the answer sheet at the end of the Listening test.

TIP The speaker will use the same place names you see in the list. These won't be paraphrased in any way.

TIP The letters on the plan are not in the same order as the places you hear mentioned, but the places in the numbered questions are.

Questions 15–20
Label the plan below.
Write the correct letter, **A–I**, next to **Questions 15–20**.

Plan of the renovated factory complex

15 Conference centre ....
16 New office space ....
17 Stores ....
18 Finance ....
19 Café ....
20 IT department ....

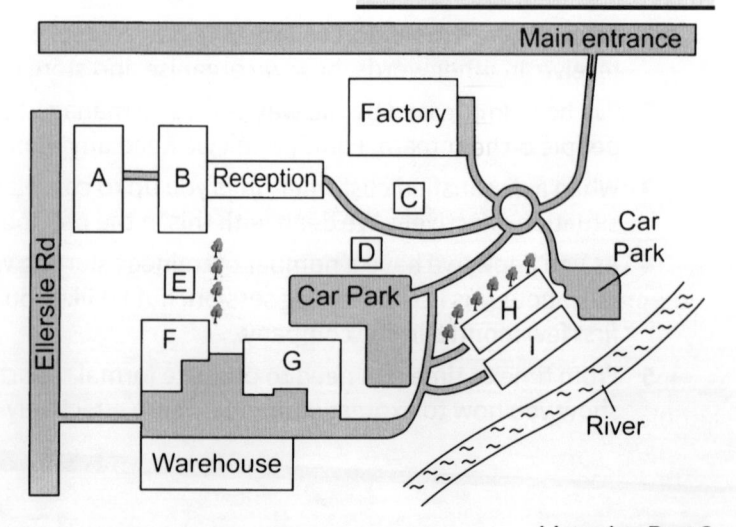

Training Test 1 — Listening Part 3

What is Listening Part 3?

- a discussion between two or sometimes three speakers (e.g. between one or more students and / or their university tutor)
- two tasks (e.g. flow-chart, multiple-choice or matching)
- 10 questions, with a brief pause in the discussion between the parts that relate to each task

The subject is an aspect of academic life (e.g. a presentation).

Task information: *3-option multiple-choice*

In Part 3, this task usually focuses on attitude / opinion, negotiation and (dis)agreement.

You have to:
- listen to the recording, which you will hear once only.
- choose from options **A**, **B** or **C** to answer a question or complete a statement so that it means the same as the information in the recording.

Useful strategy: identifying the locating words

In many IELTS tasks you need to identify the words (e.g. in the notes, flow-chart or questions) which are also in the recording. These words will help you follow a conversation and know which part of it contains the information you need.

Locating words are usually dates or statistics, names objects or events, which are difficult to paraphrase.

1 Underline the locating words in questions 1–6.

History of antibiotics

Fleming's discovery of penicillin in 1928 reduced people's fear of **1** ....

↓

pharmaceutical companies realised antibiotics like penicillin and chloramphenicol could lead to **2** ....

↓

jungles and mountain areas were explored for **3** ....

↓

manufacturers in the US and Europe decided to focus on **4** .... instead

↓

5 .... have offered a limited range of antibiotics since the 1970s

↓

some **6** .... no longer respond to antibiotics, with 700,000 cases annually

What does it test?

- identifying key facts and ideas and how they relate to each other
- identifying speakers' attitudes and opinions
- recognising agreement and disagreement

Task information: *Flow-chart completion*

Flow-chart completion requires you to follow the development of a discussion. The steps in the flow-chart are in the same order as what you hear.

You have to:
- listen to part of the discussion, which you hear once only.
- choose one option (**A**, **B**, **C**, etc.) from the box to complete each space in the flow-chart according to what you hear.

Vocabulary

For Part 3 flow-charts, the vocabulary in the options will be different to the language you hear in the recording.

1 Look at these examples of language from the recording on the history of antibiotics. Match them with options A–I.

1. the financial gain would be enormous.
2. clinics and hospitals
3. people receiving medical care
4. specimens of microorganisms
5. artificial kinds of antibiotic
6. a cut that went septic / a sore throat
7. a real improvement
8. doctors and surgeons
9. severe illness

A   synthetic forms
B   serious diseases
C   genuine progress
D   common infections
E   medical professionals
F   bacteria samples
G   treatment centres
H   sick patients
I   large profits

2 Listen to some extracts. Complete the flow-chart with options A–I. (08)

Useful strategy: *3-option multiple-choice*

For Part 3, these questions may test understanding of agreement and disagreement.
1 Look at the list of phrases.
Decide whether they suggest agreement ✓, or disagreement ✗.

1 Actually, you could be right. ☐	7 I'm not sure I go along with that. ☐
2 I doubt it. ☐	8 That's one way of looking at it, but … ☐
3 I hardly think so. ☐	9 You have a point there. ☐
4 Fair enough. ☐	10 Exactly. ☐
5 I couldn't agree more. ☐	11 Come on. Surely that's not the case. ☐
6 Precisely. ☐	12 Not necessarily. ☐

Exam Practice Test 1 — Listening Part 3

Action plan for *Flow-chart completion*

1 Read the instructions and check how many spaces there are in the flow-chart.
2 Look at the heading of the flow-chart to find out the discussion topic.
3 Look at the flow-chart and underline the locating words.
4 Read the list of options, and remember they will probably be paraphrased in the recording.
5 Listen carefully to the conversation, and be ready for the answer when you hear the locating words.
6 Transfer your answers to the answer sheet at the end of the test.

TIP The question numbers run horizontally across each row.

TIP Many of the options fit in several spaces. Don't try and guess the answers.

TIP Focus on each question in turn. As soon as you have answered one question, look at the next stage of the flow-chart.

Questions 21–26
09 Complete the flow-chart below.
Choose **SIX** answers from the box and write the correct letter, **A–I**, next to **Questions 21–26**.

A lifestyle changes
B famous people
C scientific findings
D industrial processes
E poor diet
F effective packaging
G toxic substances
H processed foods
I alarming images

Advice

A–I These options may be mentioned in any order. Three of them will not be needed.
21 Listen for the date as the answer will come shortly afterwards.
23 Governments is the locating word. **Popularity** is expressed using different language in the recording.
24 Both **1940s** and **housewives** are useful locating words.
25 How might **more accessible to consumers** be paraphrased?
26 What's another way of saying **rise**? The answer will come after one of the speakers has said this.

History of vitamin supplements

Prior to 1900s: physical weakness is thought to be caused by **21** ....
↓
Early 1900s: research shows a link between **22** .... and sickness
↓
1930s: governments become concerned about the popularity of **23** ....
↓
1940s: **24** .... convince housewives to buy vitamin supplements
↓
1950s: **25** .... make vitamin supplements more accessible to consumers
↓
1960s to present day: vitamin supplement sales continue to rise because of **26** ....

18 Exam Practice Test 1 — Listening Part 3

Action Plan for *3-option multiple-choice*

1. Read the questions. They give you an idea of what information you should listen for.
2. Underline the locating words in the questions.
3. Quickly read through the A, B, C options, remembering that these will be paraphrased in the recording.
4. As soon as you've chosen the answer to a question, listen for the answer to the next one.
5. Check your answers and transfer them to the answer sheet at the end of the Listening test.

TIP Underline locating words that are unique to each question.

Questions 27–30

Choose the correct letter, A, B or C.

27 Sam believes that more Australians are taking vitamin supplements because they
  A want to have control of their own health.
  B are advised to by local health authorities.
  C have benefitted from competition amongst manufacturers.

28 Lucy is concerned that the US vitamin supplement industry is not required to
  A follow the guidelines produced by a government agency.
  B list all the possible side effects of taking vitamins.
  C provide evidence that their products are effective.

29 When discussing the Danish experiment, Lucy and Sam conclude that vitamin supplements
  A are best used for preventing minor illnesses.
  B are not fully understood by researchers.
  C are harmful if taken in large amounts.

30 Lucy and Sam agree that stricter regulation of the vitamin supplement industry
  A would only lead to a slight decrease in sales.
  B might be necessary for some types of vitamin.
  C may not be welcomed by all consumers.

Advice

27 Choose the option that reflects Sam's personal opinion, not just an idea he refers to.

28 The options do not follow the order of the information Lucy gives.

29 *Minor illnesses*, *scientists* and *harmful* are all paraphrased in the recording. But the option you choose must exactly reflect Lucy and Sam's conclusion.

30 Listen for phrases of agreement and disagreement to help you choose the right option.

Training Test 1 — Listening Part 4

What is Listening Part 4?
- a lecture, talk or presentation given by one speaker, usually in front of an audience
- one or two tasks e.g. note completion, sentence completion
- 10 questions

The subject is a topic of academic interest (e.g. a scientific or historical subject).

What does it test?
- understanding and distinguishing between ideas: reasons, causes, effects, consequences, etc.
- following the way the ideas are organised (e.g. main ideas, specific information, attitude) and the speaker's opinion
- accurate spelling

Task information: *Sentence completion*

This task requires you to fill in the spaces in a set of sentences. It is almost identical to note completion. The sentences are in the same order as the information you hear.

For this task you have to:
- listen to a talk, once only.
- read the instructions so you know how many words you may write.
- write the exact words you hear.
- spell everything correctly.

Vocabulary: environmental issues and collocation

1 Underline the correct word in each sentence.
   1 *Habitat / Area / Land loss* is the biggest threat to wildlife in the region.
   2 The white rhino is high on the list of critically *risky / endangered / rare* species.
   3 Leftover food accounts for a high proportion of *household / dwelling / residence* waste.
   4 Governments are now investing in *recycled / renewable / reused* energy such as solar power.
   5 Don't take so many flights if you want to reduce your carbon *footprint / steps / tracks*.
   6 Vehicle *releases / productions / emissions* are largely responsible for the rise in asthma rates.
   7 Most scientists say global *heating / warming / melting* is a consequence of human activity.
   8 At some point, we will certainly run out of fossil *energies / powers / fuels*.

Useful strategy: signposting

For Part 4 lectures and talks, a speaker may sometimes use signposting language to show they are moving on to a new aspect of the topic e.g.
- 'Now let's turn to…'
- 'Moving on, let's now think about…'

The speaker may also ask a question or make a statement that
- paraphrases a subheading in the Notes.
- uses many of the same words from the subheading.

1   Read the subheadings 1–5 in the *Note completion* task below. Match the subheadings with the examples of signposting A–E. You do not need to fill the gaps.

The future of the world's trees

1 Trees and their commercial use
- We need trees for
    - construction materials
    - the .... industry

2 Trees in the ecosystem
- Trees provide a range of species with both
    - a food source
    - opportunities for ....

3 The ways that trees can affect our general happiness
- Researchers have proved that living near to trees
    - reduces the amount of .... that people have
    - encourages better relations between ....

4 The reasons why different tree species are dying out
- Diseases are often spread because
    - the restrictions on .... are not enough
    - some people ignore the rules about entering ....

5 Solutions for saving the trees
- Scientists need to share their data on ....
- Greater funding must be given to the collection of ....

Signposting examples

A   Well, there are a number of reasons why various species of tree are dying out.
B   So what can we do about this problem? There are a number of ways that ....
C   Let's think about the role trees play in the wider environment. Many birds and animals ....
D   Let's start with an overview of how trees are used by manufacturers.
E   Another way that trees are useful to us relates to the impact they have on our overall wellbeing, that is to say, how they influence our emotional health.

Useful language: cause and effect

In Part 4, the questions may test your understanding of cause and effect.

1   **Decide if the underlined phrase is followed by cause or effect.**
    1   Plastic pollution <u>has led to</u> a number of marine species being threatened.
    2   <u>Due to</u> a rise in air temperature, the polar caps are melting faster than ever before.
    3   The same fields have been used to produce crops for decades. <u>The result of this</u> has been poor soil quality.
    4   <u>Since</u> we haven't received enough funding for the project, we'll need to raise money ourselves.
    5   Organic food sales are going up <u>owing to the fact</u> that people don't want food sprayed with insecticide.
    6   Gorillas have lost much of their natural habitat, <u>meaning</u> that they are struggling to survive.

Exam Practice Test 1 — Listening Part 4

Action plan for *Sentence completion*
1. Look at the instructions and check how many words you must write in each space.
2. Read the questions (the sentences) carefully, identifying the locating words.
3. Listen and complete each space with the exact words you hear.
4. Before you transfer your answers to the answer sheet, check that the completed sentence makes sense.

TIP The locating words may appear anywhere in a question, but you will hear them before the answer in the recording.

TIP Listen out for examples of signposting that tell you when to move on to a new set of questions.

Questions 31–36
Complete the notes below.

Write **NO MORE THAN TWO WORDS** for each answer.

Insect Extinction in the 21st Century

The reasons why insect populations are declining
- In Europe, important plants are no longer found in fields or **31** ....
- In the Amazon rainforest, **32** .... might be the cause of butterfly and beetle loss.
- Globally, pesticides are affecting the spatial skills and **33** .... of bees.

The consequences of declining insect populations
- Insects are an essential part of the **34** .... in all places apart from Antarctica.
- Crop production will fall dramatically.
- Researchers can't discover any new **35** .... based on plants.

The possible ways to prevent insect extinction
- Governments must restrict the sale of pesticides.
- People must reduce their consumption of **36** ....

Questions 37–40

Complete the sentences below.

Write **ONE WORD ONLY** for each answer.

37 Sand from the Antioch Dunes was used to make .... for houses in the early 1900s.
38 The metalmark butterfly requires one type of Antioch Dunes plant for its ....
39 In recent years .... has led to the loss of wildlife in the Antioch Dunes.
40 The Antioch Dunes project shows how .... does not always require much land.

Advice
37 What kind of things do builders sometimes need to make for houses?

38 Why do butterflies need plants? Think of some different reasons.

39 You need to listen out for a cause i.e. the reason why wildlife has decreased.

40 The auxiliary **does**, and the lack of an article (a / an), shows you that the answer must be an uncountable noun.

Training Test 1 — Reading Passage 1

What is Reading Passage 1?
- a text of up to 900 words, mostly factual or descriptive
- two or three different tasks, with a total of 13 questions
- the text is slightly easier than Passages 2 and 3

Task information: *True / False / Not given*

True / False / Not given tasks require you to compare information given in a series of statements with information in the text and decide if they are the same.

You have to:
- read statements that are in the same order as the information in the text.
- scan read the text to find the part that you need.
- decide if the information in each statement agrees with the text (True), contradicts the text (False) or does not appear in the text (Not given).

Useful strategy: identifying key words and phrases

1 Look at the statements below. There is no accompanying text, but the statements include useful information even when studied on their own. Underline the key words and phrases that would show you where to look in the text. These are the 'locating words'. The first one has been done as an example.

   1 The study by <u>Canadian scientists in 2011</u> made *a surprising discovery*.
   2 A newspaper report in the Sydney Daily Times *contained factual errors*.
   3 Some academics have *criticised the theory* put forward by Dr Jonathan Purdie.
   4 Whales off the coast of South Africa *behave in the same way* as whales in New Zealand waters.
   5 The Rolls-Royce Merlin engine was *modified and improved* in its first years in production.
   6 The British public *held a wide variety of opinions on this topic*, according to a survey completed by over 3,000 people.

2 Which of the following might be used as locating words?
   - a geographical location
   - the name of an academic
   - an adverb or adjective
   - the title of a publication
   - the date of a study or survey
   - the name of a product
   - a species of animal or plant
   - prepositions and conjunctions
   - a specific nationality
   - a historic period, e.g. the 19th century

Useful strategy: identifying words with a similar meaning

1 The language used in the statements and the text will be different. To decide whether the statements are True, False or Not given, you will need to recognise **synonyms** and **paraphrases** (words and phrases with a similar meaning).

   Look at the six statements again. Match the words in italics with an option (A–F) that has a similar meaning.
   A 'However, this idea has been rejected by other scientists because…'
   B '… redesigned in order to make it more fuel efficient.'
   C '… and this was a finding that was completely unexpected.'
   D '… both groups use identical techniques to communicate with each other.'
   E '… ordinary people expressed a broad range of views…'
   F '… included statements that have since been shown to be inaccurate.'

Task information: *Table, Note, Flow-chart completion, Diagram labelling*

All of these task types require you to understand the organisational structure of one part of a text. Notes usually represent a text that is chronological or thematic. Tables represent a text that compares different items. Flow-charts represent a text that outlines a process or series of events. Diagrams represent a text that describes how something functions. The requirements for all four task types are similar.

You have to:
- scan read the text to locate the part that you need.
- find one or more words and / or a number in the text and then copy them into the space in a note or sentence.

Useful strategy: identifying locating words and phrases

Look at the extract from a set of notes below. Underline the key headings, words and phrases that would help you locate the right part of the text.

Complete the notes below.

Choose **ONE WORD ONLY** for each answer.

The Discovery of Antarctica

18th and Early 19th Centuries
- 1773: James Cook saw several rocky **1**_____ from his ship near Antarctica
- 1820: Bellingshausen and Lazarev saw the coast of Antarctica
- 1821: on an expedition to hunt **2**_____ at sea, John Davis landed in Antarctica
- 1829–31: the first **3**_____ was brought back from Antarctica

Late 19th Century
- 1895: The International Geographical Congress encouraged exploration and **4**_____ in Antarctica
- 1898: a Belgian expedition stayed in Antarctica over **5**_____
- 1898: **6**_____ were used for transport for the first time

---

Useful strategy: anticipating possible answers

1 Underline the important words before and/or after each space in the notes. What do these words tell you about the missing word?

The first one has been done for you as an example.
- 1773: James Cook saw <u>several</u> <u>rocky</u> **1**.............................. <u>from his ship near Antarctica</u>

    several: so, more than one
    rocky: so, some form of land
    from his ship near Antarctica: so, at sea, not on the continent itself

    Now follow the same procedure for 2–6 in the notes.

2 Use one word from the box to fill each space in the notes (1–6). The information you have found in Exercise 1 will help you.

| fossil | walking | winter | dogs | islands | storm | science | seals |

Why do people collect things?

People from almost every culture love collecting things. They might collect stamps, books, cards, priceless paintings or worthless ticket stubs to old sports games. Their collection might hang on the walls of a mansion or be stored in a box under the bed. So what is it that drives people to collect? Psychologist Dr Maria Richter argues that the urge to collect is a basic human characteristic. According to her, in the very first years of life we form emotional connections with lifeless objects such as soft toys. And these positive relationships are the starting point for our fascination with collecting objects. In fact, the desire to collect may go back further still. Scientists suggest that for some ancient humans living hundreds of thousands of years ago, collecting may have had a serious purpose. Only by collecting sufficient food supplies to last through freezing winters or dry summers could our ancestors stay alive until the weather improved.

It turns out that even collecting for pleasure has a very long history. In 1925, the archaeologist Leonard Woolley was working at a site in the historic Babylonian city of Ur. Woolley had travelled to the region intending only to excavate the site of a palace. Instead, to his astonishment, he dug up artefacts which appeared to belong to a 2,500-year-old museum. Among the objects was part of a statue and a piece of a local building. And accompanying some of the artefacts were descriptions like modern-day labels. These texts appeared in three languages and were carved into pieces of clay. It seems likely that this early private collection of objects was created by Princess Ennigaldi, the daughter of King Nabonidus. However, very little else is known about Princess Ennigaldi or what her motivations were for setting up her collection.

This may have been one of the first large private collections, but it was not the last. Indeed, the fashion for establishing collections really got started in Europe around 2,000 years later with the so-called 'Cabinets of Curiosities'. These were collections, usually belonging to wealthy families, that were displayed in cabinets or small rooms. Cabinets of Curiosities typically included fine paintings and drawings, but equal importance was given to exhibits from the natural world such as animal specimens, shells and plants.

Some significant private collections of this sort date from the fifteenth century. One of the first belonged to the Medici family. The Medicis became a powerful political family in Italy and later a royal house, but banking was originally the source of all their wealth. The family started by collecting coins and valuable gems, then artworks and antiques from around Europe. In 1570 a secret 'studio' was built inside the Palazzo Medici to house their growing collection. This exhibition room had solid walls without windows to keep the valuable collection safe.

In the seventeenth century, another fabulous collection was created by a Danish physician named Ole Worm. His collection room contained numerous skeletons and specimens, as well as ancient texts and a laboratory. One of Ole Worm's motivations was to point out when other researchers had made mistakes, such as the false claim that birds of paradise had no feet. He also owned a great auk, a species of bird that has now become extinct, and the illustration he produced of it has been of value to later scientists.

The passion for collecting was just as strong in the nineteenth century. Lady Charlotte Guest spoke at least six languages and became well-known for translating English books into Welsh. She also travelled widely throughout Europe acquiring old and rare pottery, which she added to her collection at home in southern England. When Lady Charlotte died in 1895 this collection was given to the Victoria and Albert Museum in London. At around the same time in the north of England, a wealthy goldsmith named Joseph Mayer was building up an enormous collection of artefacts, particularly those dug up from sites in his local area. His legacy, the Mayer Trust, continues to fund public lectures in accordance with his wishes.

In the twentieth century, the writer Beatrix Potter had a magnificent collection of books, insects, plants and other botanical specimens. Most of these were donated to London's Natural History Museum, but Beatrix held on to her cabinets of fossils, which she was particularly proud of. In the United States, President Franklin D. Roosevelt began his stamp collection as a child and continued to add to it all his life. The stress associated with being president was easier to cope with, Roosevelt said, by taking time out to focus on his collection. By the end of his life this had expanded to include model ships, coins and artworks.

Most of us will never own collections so large or valuable as these. However, the examples given here suggest that collecting is a passion that has been shared by countless people over many centuries.

Action plan for *True / False / Not given*
1 Look at the title and decide who or what the text is about.
2 Skim read the text very quickly to get an idea of the content and structure. Don't worry about words you don't understand.
3 Look at the questions and underline the locating words.
4 Find the part of the text that is relevant to the first question. Read it in detail and decide if the answer is **True**, **False** or **Not given**. Remember to look out for synonyms and paraphrases.
5 Now do the same for the other questions.

TIP The information you need for all the questions may come from one part of the text. However, sometimes there may be paragraphs that do not relate to any of the questions. The locating words in the questions will help you find the right part of the text.

Questions 1–6

Do the following statements agree with the information given in Reading Passage 1?

In boxes 1–6 on your answer sheet, write

TRUE	if the statement agrees with the information
FALSE	if the statement contradicts the information
NOT GIVEN	if there is no information on this

1 Dr Maria Richter believes that people become interested in collecting in early childhood.
2 A form of collecting may have helped some ancient humans to survive.
3 Leonard Woolley expected to find the remains of a private collection at Ur.
4 Woolley found writing that identified some of the objects he discovered.
5 Princess Ennigaldi established her collection to show off her wealth.
6 Displaying artworks was the main purpose of Cabinets of Curiosities.

Advice

1 The locating words are **Dr Maria Richter**. The information you need is in the first paragraph.

2 The locating words are **ancient humans**. You may need to read more than one sentence to find the answer. Look for synonyms or paraphrases for **survive**.

3 Find the locating words in the question. To answer the question, focus particularly on what the person **expected to find** before arriving at Ur.

4 Look for synonyms/paraphrases for **writing that identified some of the objects**.

5 What does the text say about her reasons for establishing the collection?

6 What items were displayed in most Cabinets of Curiosities? Did one type of item have higher status than others?

TIP The questions are in the same order as the information in the passage.

TIP Don't use your own knowledge of the subject to answer the questions. Use only the information in the passage.

TIP Two or more questions following each other may have the same answer.

Reading Passage 1　　　　　　　　　　　　　　Exam Practice Test 1　27

Action plan for *Note completion*

1. Look at the instructions to see how many words you must write.
2. Look at the heading of the notes – this will help you locate the relevant part of the text.
3. Study the notes carefully. Use the locating words (such as dates and proper nouns) to help you find the specific parts of the text that you need to read in detail.
4. For each question, underline the word(s) in the text which fit(s) the space. Then copy the word(s) into the notes.
5. Read the notes again carefully to make sure they make sense.

TIP The notes have a title. Use this to help you locate the relevant part of the text.

TIP You never need to change the word(s) you copy (e.g. from a noun into a verb, or from singular to plural). Make sure you spell the word(s) correctly.

Questions 7–13

Complete the notes below.

Choose **ONE WORD ONLY** *from the passage for each answer.*

Write your answers in boxes 7–13 on your answer sheet.

Some significant private collections

15th–17th Centuries
- The Medici family made their money from **7**_____
- At the Palazzo Medici there was a hidden 'studio' which had no **8**_____
- Ole Worm liked to show when other scientists had made mistakes.
- Ole Worm made an important **9**_____ of a bird.

19th Century
- Lady Charlotte Guest created a collection of **10**_____, which she left to a museum.
- Joseph Mayer paid for **11**_____ that are still given to the public today.

20th Century
- Beatrix Potter did not give away her collection of **12**_____
- Franklin D. Roosevelt believed collecting helped him deal with the **13**_____ of his job.

Advice

7 There are clear locating words here. Focus on how the family made their money, not on their other activities.

9 Focus on Worm's activities with regard to the bird, not anything else.

10 The phrase 'which she left to a museum' is important.

12 The phrase 'did not give away' is important.

TIP Read the instructions carefully. If the instructions say **ONE WORD ONLY** and you write two words, you will receive no marks, even if one of your words is the correct answer.

TIP Some parts of the notes may not have a space in them. This will help you locate the information you need in the text.

Training Test 1 — Reading Passage 2

What is Reading Passage 2?
- a text of up to 900 words
- each paragraph labelled with a letter, A, B, C, etc.
- three different tasks, with a total of 13 questions

Task information: *Matching headings*

Matching headings tasks require you to choose the correct heading for each paragraph of the text.

You have to:
- read the text, focusing on the content of each paragraph.
- read a list of possible headings. There are more headings than paragraphs.
- choose a heading for each paragraph that summarises all the information in it.

Useful strategy: identifying key words and phrases

1 Look at headings i–vi below. Underline the key words and phrases that would reflect the content of a paragraph in a text. The first one has been done for you as an example.

   i   A number of health problems associated with reading from screens
      - a number of: so, there will be three or more
      - health problems: so, some different health problems will be identified
      - reading from screens: so, the cause of the problem will be reading from screens
   ii A survey investigating the reading preferences of a range of subjects
   iii Two research experiments that reached contrasting conclusions
   iv Viewpoints of companies that manufacture electronic screens
   v   One academic who is campaigning for screens to be redesigned
   vi The way the eye gathers information and transmits it to the brain

Task information: *Matching statements with people*

Tasks involving *matching statements with people* require you to identify the views or opinions of different people mentioned in the text.

You have to:
- read a set of statements about the topic of the text.
- locate different people in the text who express a view (given in either direct or reported speech).
- match the statements with the correct person in the text.

Useful strategies: identifying words with a similar meaning

1 Match statements 1–4 with the correct option, A or B, by looking for synonyms and paraphrases.

1. *Our company has spent large sums of money investigating safety and cannot find any evidence that using our products is harmful to health.*
   - A According to Olivia Downey, her laboratory has conducted extensive research and concluded that reading from screens may cause headaches and eye problems in some people.
   - B James Rawlings says, 'Here at Household Electronics we have invested heavily in research; this shows no connection between the screens we manufacture and headaches, eye problems or other such issues.'

2. *The results of the research are not reliable because the sample size used in the study was too small.*
   - A Dr Aliya Hassan argues that because so few subjects took part in the experiment, the findings are invalid.
   - B 'It was difficult to find a large group of research subjects because the experiment required them to spend a long period away from their families,' said Professor Hamish Lannighan.

3. *It is possible to change public opinion but it will only happen as the result of making the facts and statistics widely available.*
   - A If we release the data via a broad range of different media then we will be able to alter the views of ordinary people, said eye specialist Daniel Monkman.
   - B Industry spokesperson Mei Tan claimed, 'Despite a concerted campaign using both social and print media, the attempt to influence the views of ordinary people has met with limited success.'

4. *The research done so far has been encouraging but it is still too early in the research process to draw any firm conclusions.*
   - A According to Marie Dubois, the studies that she is aware of have produced a variety of results and scientists may need to find an alternative approach.
   - B Peter Triel, a lecturer at the University of Hamilton, said, 'We won't know for sure until more work has been completed but the studies to date have returned some very positive results.'

Task information: *Summary completion*

Summary completion tasks require you to understand the main points of one part of the text.

You have to:
- identify the part of the text to which the summary refers. The summary has a title to help you do this.
- read that part of the text in detail.
- study the summary to identify what type of information is missing.
- complete the spaces in the summary using one or more words from the text.

There is also another type of summary completion task (see Test 2 Reading Passage 3).

Useful strategy: identifying what type of information is missing

1 Look at the summary below. Underline the key words and phrases that would help you identify what type of information is missing. The words around the first space have been underlined for you as an example.

- reduce the amount: so, this must be something that can be reduced or increased easily
- around your computer screen; so, this must be a common object in homes/offices
- distract your eyes: so, this must be a possible distraction

How To Avoid Eye Strain

First of all, try to <u>reduce the amount</u> of **1**_____ <u>around your computer screen</u> that might <u>distract your eyes</u>. On the screen itself, the best colour combination is **2**_____ text on a white background to provide a strong contrast. It's also important to take regular breaks and stretch your **3**_____ to reduce fatigue. Furthermore, research has shown that having a **4**_____ that is properly designed helps your posture and reduces stress-related problems such as eye strain. And finally, if you wear glasses or contact lenses, make sure your **5**_____ is correct by visiting your optometrist regularly.

2 Now use the information you underlined to choose the correct answers from the box.

| shoulders | head | black | glasses | prescription | yellow | light | workstation | examination |

Exam Practice Test 1 — Reading Passage 2

Action plan for *Matching headings*

1. Before you read the passage, read the list of headings and underline the key words.
2. Read the passage quickly to get a general idea of its content and structure.
3. Now read each paragraph carefully. Identify the writer's main point in each paragraph.
4. Look at the list of headings and choose the one that summarises the main idea.

TIP If there is a *Matching headings* task, it comes before the passage to encourage you to read the headings first.

Questions 14–19

Reading Passage 2 has six paragraphs, **A–F**.
Choose the correct heading for each paragraph from the list of headings below.
*Write the correct number, **i–viii**, in boxes 14–19 on your answer sheet.*

List of Headings

i   A contrast between two historic approaches to documentary filmmaking
ii Disagreement between two individual documentary makers
iii A wide range of opportunities to promote documentary films
iv A number of criticisms about all documentary filmmaking in the past
v   One film that represented a fresh approach to documentary filmmaking
vi Some probable future trends in documentary filmmaking
vii The debate about the origins of documentary filmmaking
viii The ability of ordinary people to create documentary films for the first time

TIP The headings in the list are in a random order. There are more headings than paragraphs. A heading can be used once only.

TIP The language used in the headings and in the passage may not be the same. Look for synonyms and paraphrases.

TIP The heading refers to the main idea throughout the paragraph, not minor details.

14 Paragraph A _____
15 Paragraph B _____
16 Paragraph C _____
17 Paragraph D _____
18 Paragraph E _____
19 Paragraph F _____

Advice

14 Pay particular attention to the paragraph structure: **Firstly**, **Secondly**, **Lastly**.
15 What is the significance of the dates in this paragraph?
16 What is the significance of the word **However** in the middle of this paragraph?
18 Why is the film *Catfish* important?

Making Documentary Films

A

For much of the twentieth century, documentary films were overshadowed by their more successful Hollywood counterparts. For a number of reasons, documentaries were frequently ignored by critics and film studies courses at universities. Firstly, the very idea of a documentary film made some people suspicious. As the critic Dr Helmut Fischer put it, 'Documentary makers might have ambitions to tell the "truth" and show only "facts" but there is no such thing as a non-fiction film. That's because, as soon as you record an incident on camera, you are altering its reality in a fundamental way'. Secondly, even supporters of documentaries could not agree on a precise definition, which did little to improve the reputation of the genre. Lastly, there were also concerns about the ethics of filming subjects without their consent, which is a necessity in many documentary films.

B

None of this prevented documentaries from being produced, though exactly when the process started is open to question. It is often claimed that *Nanook of the North* was the first documentary. Made by the American filmmaker Robert J. Flaherty in 1922, the film depicts the hard, sometimes heroic lives of native American peoples in the Canadian Arctic. *Nanook of the North* is said to have set off a trend that continued through the 1920s with the films of Dziga Vertov in the Soviet Union and works by other filmmakers around the world. However, that 1922 starting point has been disputed by supporters of an earlier date. Among this group is film historian Anthony Berwick, who argues that the genre can be traced back as early as 1895, when similar films started to appear, including newsreels, scientific films and accounts of journeys of exploration.

C

In the years following 1922, one particular style of documentary started to appear. These films adopted a serious tone while depicting the lives of actual people. Cameras were mounted on tripods and subjects rehearsed and repeated activities for the purposes of the film. British filmmaker John Grierson was an important member of this group. Grierson's career lasted nearly 40 years, beginning with *Drifters* (1929) and culminating with *I Remember, I Remember* (1968). However, by the 1960s Grierson's style of film was being rejected by the Direct Cinema movement, which wanted to produce more natural and authentic films: cameras were hand-held; no additional lighting or sound was used; and the subjects did not rehearse. According to film writer Paula Murphy, the principles and methods of Direct Cinema brought documentaries to the attention of universities and film historians as never before. Documentaries started to be recognised as a distinct genre worthy of serious scholarly analysis.

D

Starting in the 1980s, the widespread availability of first video and then digital cameras transformed filmmaking. The flexibility and low cost of these devices meant that anyone could now be a filmmaker. Amateurs working from home could compete with professionals in ways never possible before. The appearance of online film-sharing platforms in the early 2000s only increased the new possibilities for amateur filmmakers. Nonetheless, while countless amateur documentaries were being made, perhaps the most popular documentary of 2006 was still the professionally made *An Inconvenient Truth*. New cameras and digital platforms revolutionised the *making* of films. But as critic Maria Fiala has pointed out, 'The argument sometimes put forward that these innovations immediately transformed what the public expected to see in a documentary isn't entirely accurate.'

E

However, a new generation of documentary filmmakers then emerged, and with them came a new philosophy of the genre. These filmmakers moved away from highlighting political themes or urgent social issues. Instead the focus moved inwards, exploring personal lives, relationships and emotions. It could be argued that *Catfish* (2010) was a perfect example of this new trend. The film chronicles the everyday lives and interactions of the social media generation and was both a commercial and critical success. Filmmaker Josh Camberwell maintains that *Catfish* embodies a new realisation that documentaries are inherently subjective and that this should be celebrated. Says Camberwell, 'It is a requirement for documentary makers to express a particular viewpoint and give personal responses to the material they are recording.'

F

The popularity and variety of documentaries today is illustrated by the large number of film festivals focusing on the genre around the world. The biggest of all must be the Hot Docs Festival in Canada, which over the years has showcased hundreds of documentaries from more than 50 different countries. Even older is the Hamburg International Short Film Festival. As its name suggests, Hamburg specialises in short films, but one category takes this to its limits – entries may not exceed three minutes in duration. The Short and Sweet Festival is a slightly smaller event held in Utah, USA. The small size of the festival means that for first timers this is the ideal venue to try to get some recognition for their films. Then there is the Atlanta Shortsfest, which is a great event for a wide variety of filmmakers. Atlanta welcomes all established types of documentaries and recognises the growing popularity of animations, with a category specifically for films of this type. These are just a few of the scores of film festivals on offer, and there are more being established every year. All in all, it has never been easier for documentary makers to get their films in front of an audience.

Action plan for *Matching statements with people*

1. Look at the list of names and locate them in the text.
2. For each name, read all the things that person said. This may be in direct or reported speech.
3. Match the statement with the correct person. Look for synonyms and paraphrases.

TIP It is possible that one person will make two different statements.

TIP Sometimes the statements will be listed in the box and the names will be next to the question numbers. Follow the same action plan in both cases.

TIP Sometimes the names will appear in more than one place.

TIP There may be more people than statements and one or more of the names will not be used.

Questions 20–23

Look at the statements (Questions 20–23) and the list of people below.

*Match each statement with the correct person, **A–E**.*

*Write the correct letter, **A–E**, in boxes 20–23 on your answer sheet.*

20 The creation of some new technologies did not change viewers' attitudes towards documentaries as quickly as is sometimes proposed.

21 One set of beliefs and techniques helped to make documentary films academically respectable.

22 The action of putting material on film essentially changes the nature of the original material.

23 Documentary filmmakers have an obligation to include their own opinions about and analysis of the real events that they show in their films.

List of People
A Dr Helmut Fischer
B Anthony Berwick
C Paula Murphy
D Maria Fiala
E Josh Camberwell

Advice

20 *This is about change in the attitudes of viewers, not in the way documentaries were made.*

22 *Look for a person who challenges the whole idea of a documentary film.*

Action plan for *Summary completion*

1. Read the instructions carefully. How many words and / or numbers can you use to fill each space?
2. Look at the title of the summary. This will help you locate the relevant part of the passage.
3. Underline the locating words in the summary. They will help you find exactly the right part of the passage to read in detail.
4. Compare the language around each space in the summary with the language in the passage. Look for synonyms and paraphrases.
5 Transfer the relevant information from the passage into each space and then read the summary again. It should make sense and summarise the passage.

TIP The information you need may be in one paragraph or it may be spread over a longer part of the passage.

TIP Write the words exactly as they appear in the passage. Check for singular or plural.

TIP Don't leave any spaces blank. You don't lose marks for wrong answers.

Questions 24–26

Complete the summary below.

Choose **NO MORE THAN TWO WORDS AND A NUMBER** from the passage for each answer.

Write your answers in boxes 24–26 on your answer sheet.

Film Festivals

There are many festivals for documentary makers. For example, Canada's Hot Docs festival has screened documentaries from more than 50 countries. Meanwhile, the Hamburg Short Film Festival lives up to its name by accepting films no more than **24**_____ long in one of its categories. The Short and Sweet Film Festival is especially good for documentary makers who are **25**_____. And the Atlanta Shortsfest accepts numerous forms of documentaries including **26**_____, which are becoming more common.

Advice

24 The focus here is not just short films, but extremely short films.
25 Who / What is this festival especially good for?
26 Look for one type of film among many other types.

Training Test 1 — Reading Passage 3

What is Reading Passage 3?
- a text of up to 950 words
- a discursive text that is slightly more challenging than Passages 1 and 2
- three different tasks, with a total of 14 questions

Task information: *4-option multiple-choice*

These tasks require a detailed understanding of one longer section of the passage. The questions usually refer to a longer section of the passage, often a whole paragraph. Occasionally the final question will refer to the whole passage.

You have to:
- read questions or incomplete sentences which help you locate the relevant part of the passage.
- choose the correct option, A, B, C or D, to answer the question or complete the sentence so that it means the same as the passage.

Useful strategy: recognising distraction

Only one of the four options A–D is the correct answer. However, there might be something in the passage to make you think one of the other options is the correct answer. This is called 'distraction'.

1 **Read the paragraph below about setting up a new business. Then look at the multiple-choice question and decide which is the correct answer, A, B, C or D.**

> There is no question that it is exciting to set up a new business, but it is also a time when there are numerous problems to overcome. As a business analyst, I have often seen people making the same errors. One frequent issue is that business owners try to do everything themselves because they feel a sense of responsibility; however, they should be delegating some tasks to others. Secondly, in my experience, too many new business owners do not have a comprehensive financial plan. And lastly, many of them have not studied the market thoroughly enough. All of these errors can be avoided.

What is the writer doing in the paragraph?

A suggesting some reasons why people set up a business
B explaining why her own business has been successful
C comparing the approaches of two new businesses
D outlining common mistakes made when setting up a business

2 **Now think about the three options that are incorrect. There is something in the passage that might make you *think* these are the correct answer. For each of the incorrect options, underline this distraction.**

Task information: *Matching sentence endings*

Matching sentence endings tasks require you to understand a number of important ideas expressed in the passage.

You have to:
- read the first halves of sentences. These are in the same order as the information in the passage.
- use locating words in the sentence beginnings to find the relevant parts of the passage.
- read those parts of the passage carefully to understand the idea(s) being expressed.
- choose the correct second half of the sentence from the options in a box for each question.

Useful strategy: locating the relevant part of the passage

The information you need to match all the sentences is usually located throughout the passage, which can make this task challenging. However, clear locating words are used in the sentence beginning to help you locate the relevant part of the passage.

1 **Look at these sentence beginnings. Underline the locating words / phrases that would help you find the relevant part of the passage.**
   1 Researchers working in Norway and the Arctic have shown that
   2 The use of DNA sequencing and isotope analysis has proved that
   3 Research into 'upside-down jellyfish' showed that
   4 Following research in the Mediterranean Sea it has been claimed that

Jellyfish: A Remarkable Marine Life Form

When viewed in the wild, jellyfish are perhaps the most graceful and vividly coloured of all sea creatures. But few people have ever seen a jellyfish living in its natural habitat. Instead, they might see a dead and shapeless specimen lying on the beach, or perhaps receive a painful sting while swimming, so it is inevitable that jellyfish are often considered ugly and possibly dangerous. This misunderstanding can be partly traced back to the 20th century, when the use of massive nets and mechanical winches often damaged the delicate jellyfish that scientists managed to recover. As a result, disappointingly little research was carried out into jellyfish, as marine biologists took the easy option and focused on physically stronger species such as fish, crabs and shrimp. Fortunately, however, new techniques are now being developed. For example, scientists have discovered that sound bounces harmlessly off jellyfish, so in the Arctic and Norway researchers are using sonar to monitor jellyfish beneath the ocean's surface. This, together with aeroplane surveys, satellite imagery and underwater cameras, has provided a wealth of new information in recent years.

Scientists now believe that in shallow water alone there are at least 38 million tonnes of jellyfish and that these creatures inhabit every type of marine habitat, including deep water. Furthermore, jellyfish were once regarded as relatively solitary, but this is another area where the science has evolved. Dr Karen Hansen was the first to suggest that jellyfish are in fact the centre of entire ecosystems, as shrimp, lobster and fish shelter and feed among their tentacles. This proposition has subsequently been conclusively proven by independent studies. DNA sequencing and isotope analysis have provided further insights, including the identification of numerous additional species of jellyfish unknown to science only a few years ago.

This brings us to the issue of climate change. Research studies around the world have recorded a massive growth in jellyfish populations in recent years and some scientists have linked this to climate change. However, while this may be credible, it cannot be established with certainty as other factors might be involved. Related to this was the longstanding academic belief that jellyfish had no predators and therefore there was no natural process to limit their numbers. However, observations made by Paul Dewar and his team showed that this was incorrect. As a result, the scientific community now recognises that species including sharks, tuna, swordfish and some salmon all prey on jellyfish.

It is still widely assumed that jellyfish are among the simplest lifeforms, as they have no brain or central nervous system. While this is true, we now know they possess senses that allow them to see, feel and interact with their environment in subtle ways. What is more, analysis of the so-called 'upside-down jellyfish' shows that they shut down their bodies and rest in much the same way that humans do at night, something once widely believed to be impossible for jellyfish. Furthermore, far from 'floating' in the water as they are still sometimes thought to do, analysis has shown jellyfish to be the most economical swimmers in the animal kingdom. In short, scientific progress in recent years has shown that many of our established beliefs about jellyfish were inaccurate.

Jellyfish, though, are not harmless. Their sting can cause a serious allergic reaction in some people and large outbreaks of them – known as 'blooms' – can damage tourist businesses, break fishing nets, overwhelm fish farms and block industrial cooling pipes. On the other hand, jellyfish are a source of medical collagen used in surgery and wound dressings. In addition, a particular protein taken from jellyfish has been used in over 30,000 scientific studies of serious diseases such as Alzheimer's. Thus, our relationship with jellyfish is complex as there are a range of conflicting factors to consider.

Jellyfish have existed more or less unchanged for at least 500 million years. Scientists recognise that over the planet's history there have been three major extinction events connected with changing environmental conditions. Together, these destroyed 99% of all life, but jellyfish lived through all three. Research in the Mediterranean Sea has now shown, remarkably, that in old age and on the point of death, certain jellyfish are able to revert to an earlier physical state, leading to the assertion that they are immortal. While this may not technically be true, it is certainly an extraordinary discovery. What is more, the oceans today contain 30% more poisonous acid than they did 100 years ago, causing problems for numerous species, but not jellyfish, which may even thrive in more acidic waters. Jellyfish throughout their long history have shown themselves to be remarkably resilient.

Studies of jellyfish in the class known as scyphozoa have shown a lifecycle of three distinct phases. First, thousands of babies known as planulae are released. Then, after a few days the planulae develop into polyps – stationary lifeforms that feed off floating particles. Finally, these are transformed into something that looks like a stack of pancakes, each of which is a tiny jellyfish. It is now understood that all species of jellyfish go through similarly distinct stages of life. This is further evidence of just how sophisticated and unusual these lifeforms are.

Action plan for Yes / No / Not given

1. Read the passage once quickly to get a general idea of the content and structure. Don't worry about words you don't understand at this stage.
2. Look at the view / claim in the first question. Use the locating words to find the relevant part of the passage.
3. Read that part of the passage carefully and compare it with the question. Look for synonyms and paraphrases.
4. Decide if the view / claim in the question agrees with what the writer says in the passage. Choose **Yes**, **No** or **Not given**.
5. Do the same for the other views / claims.

TIP The views / claims in the questions are in the same order as the information in the passage.

TIP Remember, it is the writer's views you need to check, not your own.

TIP Even *Not given* questions will have a clear locating word / phrase to help you find the relevant part of the passage.

Questions 27–32

Do the following statements agree with the claims of the writer in Reading Passage 3?

In boxes 27–32 on your answer sheet, write

- **YES** if the statement agrees with the claims of the writer
- **NO** if the statement contradicts the claims of the writer
- **NOT GIVEN** if it is impossible to say what the writer thinks about this

27 It is surprising that many people have negative views of jellyfish.
28 In the 20th century, scientists should have conducted more studies of jellyfish.
29 Some jellyfish species that used to live in shallow water may be moving to deep water.
30 Dr Karen Hansen's views about jellyfish need to be confirmed by additional research.
31 It is possible to reverse the consequences of climate change.
32 The research findings of Paul Dewar have been accepted by other academics.

Advice

27 Locate the 'negative views' about jellyfish in the first sentences of the passage. Is the writer surprised?

28 Which words in the question tell you about the writer's view or attitude?

30 Read the passage and decide what Dr Hansen found. What is the writer's view of Dr Hansen's research?

31 Focus on the meaning of 'reverse the consequences' of climate change. What does the writer say about this?

Action plan for *4-option multiple-choice*

1. Read the first question and the four options, A–D.
2. Find the relevant part of the passage and read it in detail. This may mean reading a whole paragraph carefully.
3. Consider all four options and choose the one you believe to be correct.
4. Follow the same plan for the rest of the questions.

TIP Multiple-choice questions follow the order of information in the text.

TIP The questions and the passage may use different language. Look out for synonyms and paraphrases.

TIP There may be distraction in the passage which makes an incorrect option seem possible.

TIP If the multiple-choice questions are the first task for the passage, read the whole passage through before you follow this plan so that you have a general idea of the content and structure of the text.

Questions 33–36

*Choose the correct letter, **A**, **B**, **C** or **D**.*
Write the correct letter in boxes 33–36 on your answer sheet.

33 What is the writer doing in the fourth paragraph?
  A comparing several different types of jellyfish
  B dismissing some common ideas about jellyfish
  C contrasting various early theories about jellyfish
  D rejecting some scientific findings regarding jellyfish

34 What does the writer conclude in the fifth paragraph?
  A Jellyfish have advantages and disadvantages for humans.
  B Humans have had a serious negative impact on jellyfish.
  C Jellyfish will cause problems for humans in the future.
  D Humans and jellyfish are fundamentally similar.

35 What is the writer's main point in the sixth paragraph?
  A Jellyfish may once have inhabited dry land.
  B Jellyfish improve the environment they live in.
  C Jellyfish have proved able to survive over time.
  D Jellyfish have caused other species to become endangered.

36 The writer refers to the 'scyphozoa' in order to
  A exemplify the great size of some jellyfish.
  B illustrate that jellyfish are biologically complex.
  C explain why certain jellyfish may become extinct.
  D suggest that scientists still misunderstand jellyfish.

Advice

33 Focus on the whole of the fourth paragraph, not just some of the content. What is the writer's purpose or intention in writing this paragraph?

34 The question asks about the writer's conclusion. But you will need to read the whole paragraph in order to fully understand the concluding sentence.

35 Identify the main point in the paragraph, not just any point in it.

36 The question is not asking what a scyphozoa is. It is asking why the writer has included this information.

Reading Passage 3   Exam Practice Test 1

Action plan for *Matching sentence endings*

1. Read the first incomplete sentence and locate the relevant part of the text.
2. Read that part of the passage carefully and compare it with the options in the box.
3. Match one of the options with the information in the passage. Look out for the use of synonyms and paraphrases.
4. After matching two parts of a sentence, read the whole sentence through. Does it reflect the writer's views / claims accurately?
5. Follow this plan for the other incomplete sentences.

TIP The incomplete sentences contain clear locating words to help you find the relevant part of the passage.

TIP If matching sentence endings is the first task for the passage, read the passage through before you follow this plan so that you have a general idea of the content and structure of the text.

TIP There will be two or three options which do not match any of the incomplete sentences, but be careful because distraction may make them seem possible.

TIP The incomplete sentences may refer to different paragraphs in the text.

Questions 37–40

Complete each sentence with the correct ending, **A–F**, below.

Write the correct letter, **A–F**, in boxes 37–40 on your answer sheet.

37 Researchers working in Norway and the Arctic have shown that
38 The use of DNA sequencing and isotope analysis has proved that
39 Research into 'upside-down jellyfish' showed that
40 Following research in the Mediterranean Sea, it has been claimed that

TIP The incomplete sentences follow the order of information in the text.

TIP The options in the box are in random order.

> A it was wrong to assume that jellyfish do not sleep.
> B certain species of jellyfish have changed their usual diet.
> C jellyfish can be observed and tracked in ways that do not injure them.
> D one particular type of jellyfish may be able to live forever.
> E there are more types of jellyfish than previously realised.
> F some jellyfish are more dangerous to humans than once thought.

Advice

37 How is today's research in Norway and the Arctic different from 20th-century research?
38 Look out for the use of synonyms and paraphrases.
40 The words 'it has been claimed' are important here. The 'claim' might not be strictly true.

Training Test 1 — Writing Task 1

What is Writing Task 1?
- A writing task based on data. This can show statistical data presented in a graph, table or chart, or it can show visual data in plans / maps or a process diagram. Sometimes more than one set of data will be included.

What does it test?
- the clear organisation of your ideas
- the ability to write an overview of what the data shows
- the ability to express the information concisely and accurately
- the use of an appropriate academic style (formal or neutral) and a range of appropriate vocabulary and grammatical structures
- accurate grammar, spelling and punctuation

Task information
Writing Task 1 requires you to recognise and select important elements from the data and summarise key points.

You have to:
- plan, write and check your work in 20 minutes.
- write a descriptive summary in at least 150 words.
- give an overview of the data in a single sentence – usually at the beginning or the end of your answer.
- write about the most important parts of the data.
- draw attention to relevant features of the data and interpret them.
- make comparisons and contrasts where relevant.

STRATEGIES

Before you write

A Reading the question

Read the task below. This is an example of a *Comparison of plans / maps task* which you might see in Writing Task 1. Think about the questions in boxes 1–3.

> **1** What does the **first sentence** in bold in the task tell you? Do the plans show two different areas or the same area at two different times? What three things does the **second sentence** remind you to do?

You should spend 20 minutes on this task.

The plans below show a science park in 2008 and the same science park today.

Summarise the information by selecting and reporting the main features, and make comparisons where relevant.

Write at least 150 words.

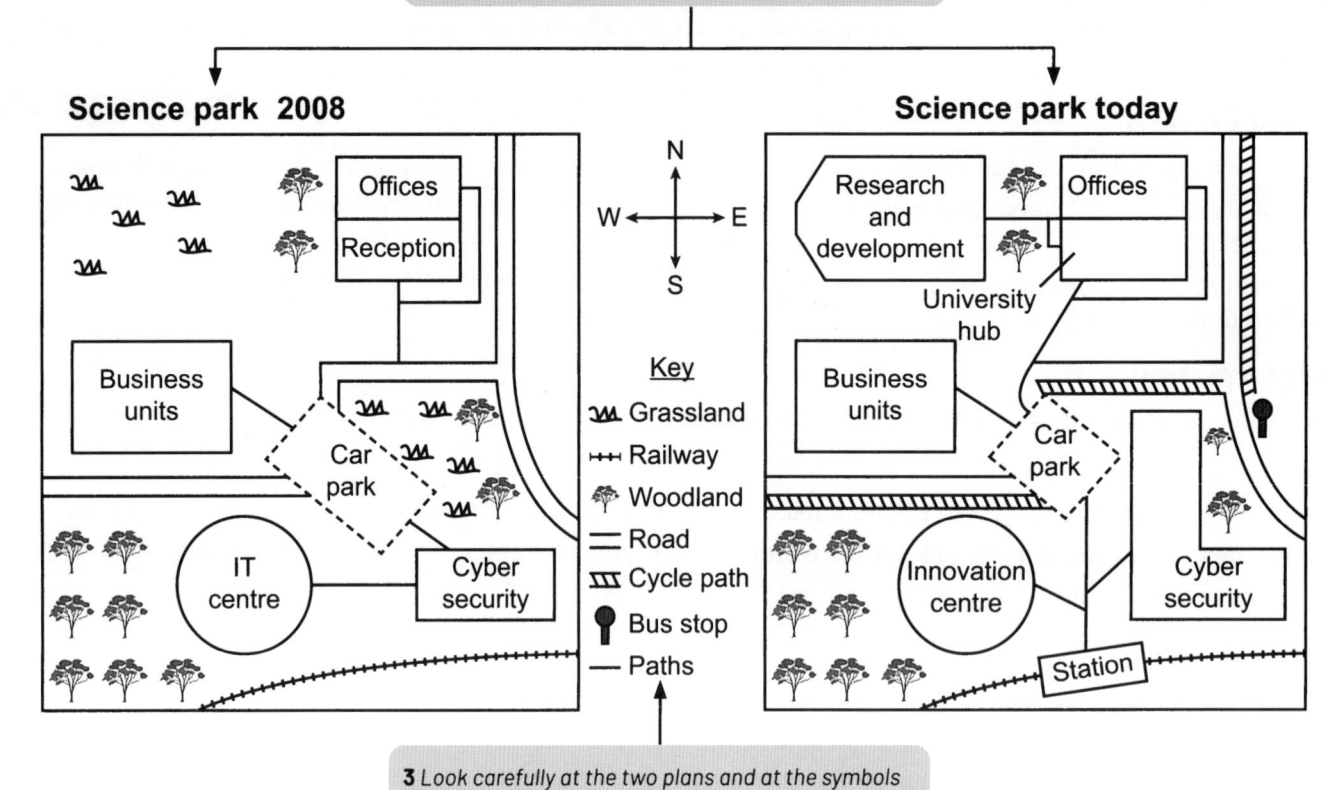

2 *Read the **title** carefully – it gives key information about the purpose of the graphic. Write a paraphrase of the title. Express the information in the title in different words to show you understand it.*

Science park 2008

Science park today

Key
- Grassland
- Railway
- Woodland
- Road
- Cycle path
- Bus stop
- Paths

3 *Look carefully at the two plans and at the symbols listed in the **Key**. Make sure you understand what each symbol means, and find an example of each symbol on the plans.*

B Understanding the data

Read the following statements about the two plans. Which of them report the data correctly? Mark them ✓ (correct) or ✗ (incorrect). Explain why the incorrect statements are wrong and correct them.

1. The plans show that since 2008, the number of roads has been increased.
2. There is now one additional building in the science park aside from the station.
3. A number of major changes have been made to the science park in the period since 2008.
4. Reception is now called offices.
5. There has been no change in the position of the railway line.
6. According to the plans, the area of grassland has expanded significantly.
7. There is now more space devoted to cyber security than in 2008.
8. The plans show that since 2008, cycle paths have has been added.

What to include in Task 1

For Task 1, you are required to write a *description* of what you see: this must be uncontroversial and evident to everyone who looks at the graphic. Where relevant, you are encouraged to make *connections* between different parts of the data, and to recognise *broad trends* and use these as the basis of your comparison.

However, there are a number of things you should avoid:
- Do not *speculate* about the reasons behind the data.
- Do not draw *inferences*.
- Do not make *evaluations*.

Look at the following sentences. Which of them do you think are valid points to make in a Task 1 answer, and which should you avoid? Why?

a The northern part of the area has seen the largest number of changes.
b A lot of money must have been spent to bring a railway station to the science park.
c The reduced number of car-parking spaces will be beneficial for the environment.
d The area covered in trees is approximately the same as in 2008.
e The reception was probably built near the road in order to facilitate access for disabled employees.
f The term **Innovation Centre** is more modern than **IT Centre**.

TIP In 150 words you cannot include a detailed description of all the changes, so you must decide which parts it is important for the reader to know and in how much detail. Decide which points to summarise, which to group together and which parts to ignore.

Selecting from the data

Take some time to look carefully at the two plans and decide what should be included in your answer.

On Plan B, circle and tick (✓) the parts which have changed since 2008. Put an equals sign (=) by elements which have not changed. Put a cross (✗) by any changes you think should be ignored because they are superficial differences.

Then decide which points you think are most important to write about. Number these in order of importance.

Orientation in Task 1

Which of these two sentences do you think would be a better way of expressing a key point? Why?

a In 2008 there were four main buildings in the science park and in the present day there are five.
b Since 2008, the number of main buildings in the science park has increased from four to five.

TIP The plans are presented to show the way an area has developed, so the focus of your summary should be on the present day and how things have changed.

Writing Task 1   Training Test 1   45

Writing a clear summary

Fill in the spaces in the sample answer with appropriate words from the box.

The two plans show changes to a science park since 2008. The most striking alteration has been to the northern part of the area, **1**_____ a Research and Development block has been constructed on the grassland, **2**_____ it is noticeable that the area covered by trees has remained approximately the same. Two buildings have been expanded, most obviously the Cyber Security unit, **3**_____ has almost doubled in size. Another important change has been to the transport arrangements. The amount of space for cars has been significantly reduced, with car parking cut by almost half. At the **4**_____ time, public transport links have been increased: a train station has been added and there is now a bus stop opposite the entrance; a cycling lane has **5**_____ been introduced. Two buildings have been given different names: the old Reception block is now called the University Hub and the IT Centre has been renamed the Innovation Centre. Taken as a **6**_____, the Science Park has undergone a number of major alterations since 2008.	**a** which **b** though **c** same **d** also **e** whole **f** where

Underline the overview sentence

In Task 1 you are encouraged to recognise connections and trends in the data. In the sample task above, underline the overview sentence and highlight the ways the writer has grouped together the changes.

Avoiding repetition: nouns and adjectives

In the sample answer, the writer has made an effort to avoid repeating vocabulary. Find at least one synonym (word or phrase) in the text for the following words:

1 obvious (adjective)
2 change (noun)
3 built (verb)
4 important (adjective)
5 introduced (verb)
6 renamed (verb)

After you write

Check through what you have written and pay special attention to errors you commonly make.

Useful language: signalling order of importance

⊚   Look at the following extracts from candidates' essays. There is an error in each sentence. Identify and correct the error.

a The most significantly change is in the size of the buildings.
b Two buildings have been changed making them noticeable larger.
c Another thing obvious is the reduction in grassland.
d The most clearest alteration in the transport is fewer cars.
e Transport links are more than in the past.

Verb forms: present perfect and present perfect passive

1 Read the sample answer to Task 1 below.

   Underline the following verb forms in the sample answer.
   a Present perfect
   b Present perfect passive

   Consider why each form is used.

> **Sample answer**
>
> The two plans show changes to a science park since 2008. The most striking alteration has been to the northern part of the area, where a Research and Development block has been constructed on the grassland, though it is noticeable that the area covered by trees has remained approximately the same. Two buildings have been expanded, most obviously the Cyber Security unit, which has almost doubled in size. Another important change has been to the transport arrangements. The amount of space for cars has been significantly reduced, with car parking cut by almost half. At the same time, public transport links have been increased: a train station has been added and there is now a bus stop opposite the entrance; a cycling lane has also been introduced. Two buildings have been given different names: the old Reception block is now called the University Hub and the IT Centre has been renamed the Innovation Centre. Taken as a whole, the Science Park has undergone a number of major alterations since 2008.

Verb forms: past simple vs present perfect

2 Look at the following sentences taken from other IELTS *Comparison of plans / maps* tasks.

   Underline the time reference and choose which verb form to use in each case.
   a Between 2015 and the beginning of 2017, eight new lecture rooms *were / have been* built.
   b The entrance to the research facility *has been / was* widened and now extends along the building.
   c Since 2010 a number of changes *were / have been* made to the design of the library.
   d In the last decade the amount of land used for wheat *has been / was* reduced.
   e After 1960, almost all of the parkland *was / has been* built on.

3 Complete the sentences with a phrase, using past simple or present perfect with the verb in brackets.
   a Since the 1980s, the number of university places for women .... (rise).
   b In the last 50 years there .... a massive increase in carbon emissions (be).
   c 27% of the rural population of the region .... (move) to urban areas after the drought.
   d Between 1970 and 2010, virtually one third of the schools in this area .... (close).

> **Advice**
>
> Sometimes tasks show two plans from the past, for example 1990 and 2010. In this case you must use the past simple rather than the present perfect.

Verb forms: Verbs to describe change

The main focus of this IELTS Comparison of plans / maps task is to describe change to an area or place. Several verbs have been used in the sample answer to indicate the **type** of change.

These are the main types of change:
- Extending
- Growing
- Making
- Adding
- Converting
- Developing
- Making less
- Staying the same

4 Look at the sample answer on page 47. Underline words which express some of these different types of change and add them to the word maps below.

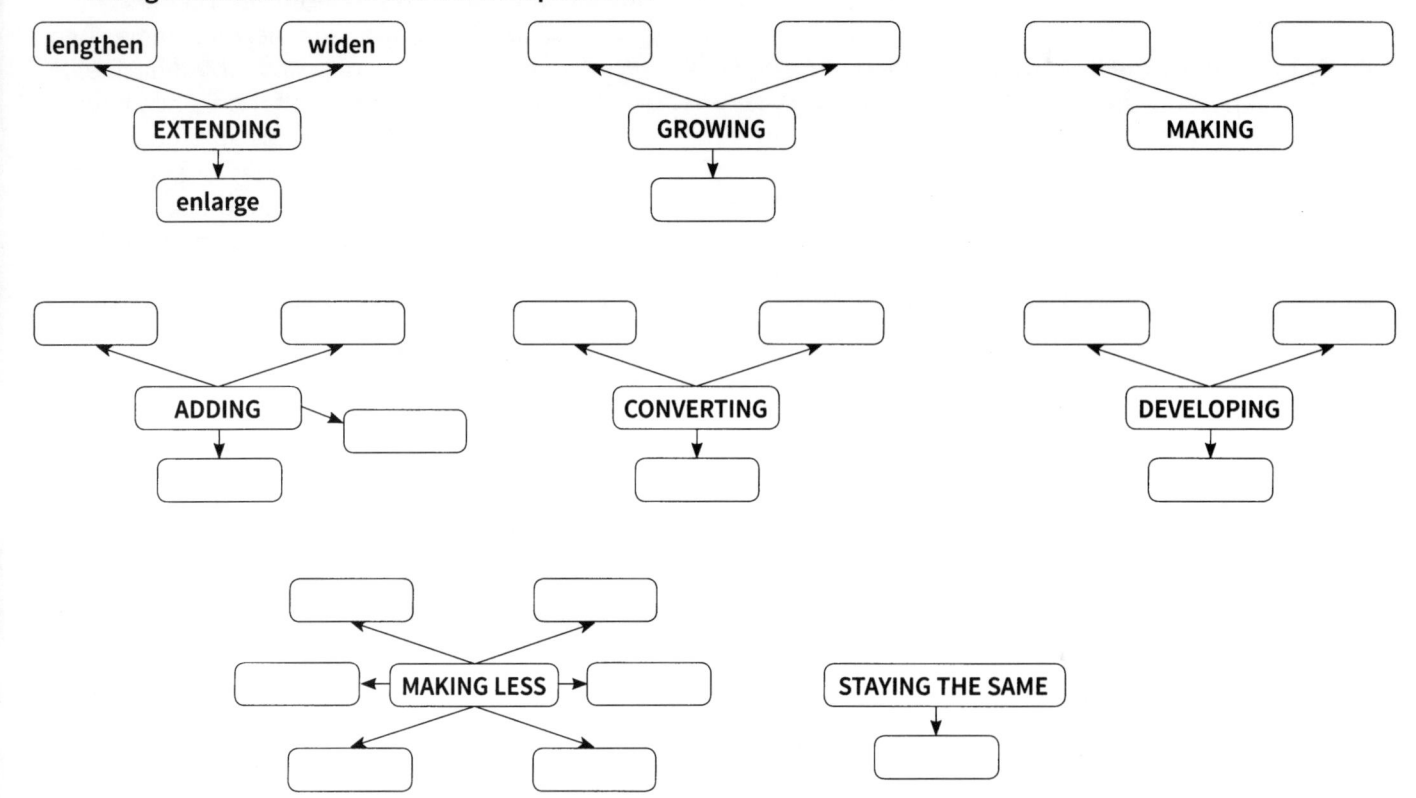

[Word maps with the following filled entries:]
- EXTENDING: lengthen, widen, enlarge
- GROWING: (blank)
- MAKING: (blank)
- ADDING: (blank)
- CONVERTING: (blank)
- DEVELOPING: (blank)
- MAKING LESS: (blank)
- STAYING THE SAME: (blank)

5 Now add the words from the box below to the word maps. Some words can be used more than once.

improve	remain	grow	widen	transfer
decline	make better	drop	build	lengthen
alter	enlarge	change	shrink	decrease

6 Which of these words:
   a ... can only be used for numbers?
   b ... can only be used for dimensions?
   c ... can be used for both numbers and dimensions?

Advice

*You cannot use **grow** in the passive except when describing plants.*

Exam Practice Test 1 — Writing Task 1

Time management is crucial in the IELTS writing exam. You are given 60 minutes to write two tasks but Task 1 is shorter and generally less complex than Task 2 (150 words compared with 250). For this reason, take no more than 20 minutes to do Task 1 to leave yourself enough time for Writing Task 2.

TIP As you do more practice of the different IELTS writing tasks, you will need less time to complete them. For the first practice attempt you should take longer for each stage (for example, 40 minutes for Task 1). In particular, give yourself plenty of time to look at the data and decide what to include in your answer before starting to write.

Action plan for *Comparison of plans/maps tasks*

Before you write

1. Look at the task on page 50 and read the question carefully. It is similar to the task on page 43 but there are important differences: you will need to think carefully about the content of the plans and which verb form to use.
2. What is the date of the first plan? What does the second plan show? Which verb form do you use to explain *these* changes: present perfect or past simple?
3. Look in detail at the plans and compare them. Make sure you understand the symbols in the Key. Decide which points you will include.
4. Make notes on what you want to include in the different parts of your text:

Opening statement	
Main comparisons (aim for at least three)	
Overview sentence	
Conclusion, if necessary	

After you write

5. Read through what you have written.
6. Check for:

Meaning

- Is it a *description* of what can be seen in the plans (not making inferences or evaluative judgements, or speculating)?
- Have you *emphasised* important points?
- Have you given an *overview* at some point in your answer? It is usually best to put this in the first or last sentence of the essay.
- Is what you have written *clear*? This is probably the most important thing to check.

Grammar

- Is the correct *verb form* used for the task?
- Do your verbs *agree with* their subjects?
- Have you used *passive and active forms* appropriately?
- Have you used correct *articles* – *a*, *the* or zero?

Spelling
- Check the spelling of your *whole* answer.
- Make sure that you have *copied* words from the graphic correctly.
- Pay particular attention to words you have *recently learned*.
- Check words with *double letters* – have you used them correctly?
- Is your *punctuation* correct? Are capital letters at the beginning of sentences clear?

Length
- Is your whole text at least *150 words* long?

Style
- Is the style *appropriate* for an academic task (formal or semi-formal)?
- Have you used *full forms* rather than contractions (for example, 'They have' rather than 'They've')?

7 Correct any mistakes you see but don't rewrite the whole essay.

Writing Task 1

You should spend 20 minutes on this task.

The plans below show the layout of the ground floor of a museum in 1990 and in 2010.

Summarise the information by selecting and reporting the main features, and make comparisons where relevant.

Write at least 150 words.

Ground floor of museum 1990 and 2010

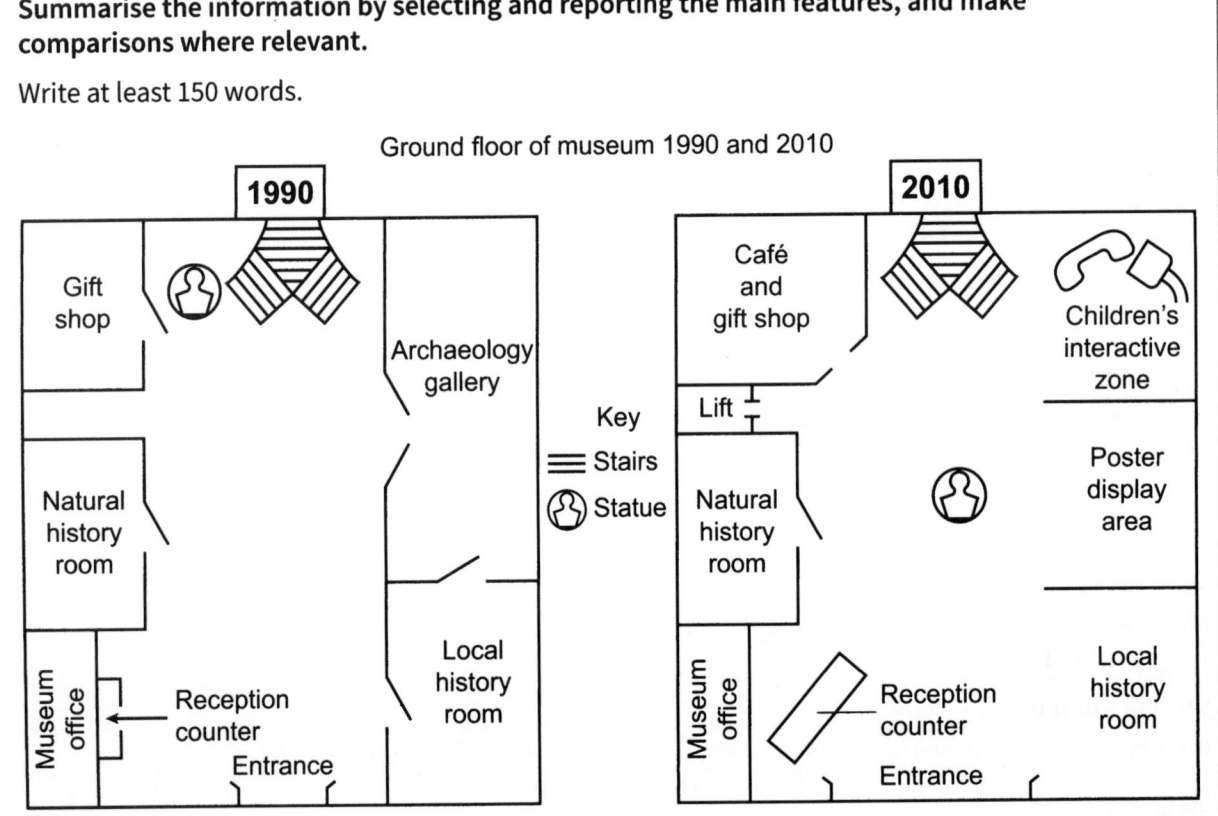

Key
= Stairs
☺ Statue

1990 layout:
- Gift shop
- Archaeology gallery
- Natural history room
- Museum office
- Reception counter
- Local history room
- Entrance

2010 layout:
- Café and gift shop
- Lift
- Children's interactive zone
- Natural history room
- Poster display area
- Museum office
- Reception counter
- Local history room
- Entrance

Training Test 1 — Writing Task 2

What is Writing Task 2?
- A formal discussion and / or argument essay

What does it test?
- the expression and evaluation of ideas
- the ability to set out clearly your own position (opinion) on the issue
- the ability to formulate and develop arguments clearly
- the use of an appropriate style, including a wide range of vocabulary and grammatical structures
- grammar, spelling and punctuation
- paragraphing

Task information
This task requires you to present arguments in a clear, persuasive and well-organised way.

You have to:
- write at least 250 words in 40 minutes.
- discuss the idea presented in the opening statement of the task (where appropriate, presenting different points of view as well).
- support your points with relevant examples.
- formulate and develop your arguments clearly.
- give a clear statement of your own opinion or position on the matter.
- formulate and develop your arguments clearly.

Useful strategies: Before you write

A Reading the question

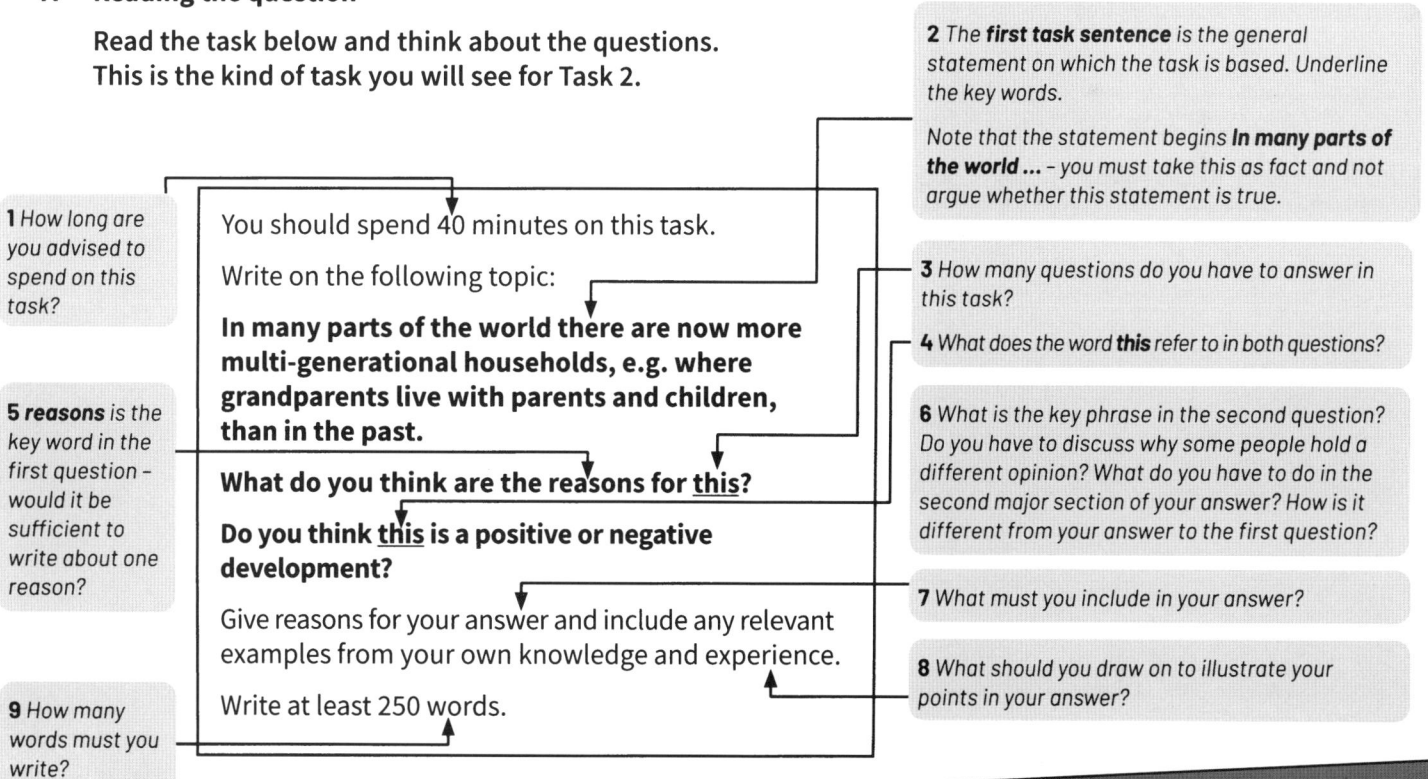

Read the task below and think about the questions. This is the kind of task you will see for Task 2.

---

1 How long are you advised to spend on this task?

You should spend 40 minutes on this task.

Write on the following topic:

In many parts of the world there are now more multi-generational households, e.g. where grandparents live with parents and children, than in the past.

What do you think are the reasons for this?

Do you think this is a positive or negative development?

Give reasons for your answer and include any relevant examples from your own knowledge and experience.

Write at least 250 words.

---

2 The **first task sentence** is the general statement on which the task is based. Underline the key words.

Note that the statement begins **In many parts of the world ...** – you must take this as fact and not argue whether this statement is true.

3 How many questions do you have to answer in this task?

4 What does the word **this** refer to in both questions?

5 reasons is the key word in the first question – would it be sufficient to write about one reason?

6 What is the key phrase in the second question? Do you have to discuss why some people hold a different opinion? What do you have to do in the second major section of your answer? How is it different from your answer to the first question?

7 What must you include in your answer?

8 What should you draw on to illustrate your points in your answer?

9 How many words must you write?

B Planning your answer

Before you start writing your answer, it is essential to plan what you want to say and to organise your points. This is one way of presenting your essay for the task on page 51 (but remember there are other ways of organising your essay which may work just as well).

> **Stage 1** An **introduction** which gives a clearer explanation of the trend explained in the first task sentence, giving a brief reaction to it
> **Stage 2** A **discussion** of the possible reasons for the trend
> **Stage 3** Your own **view** of whether this is a positive or negative trend
> **Stage 4** Your **concluding remarks**

Match these notes for Writing Task 2 on page 51 with Stages 1–4 above.

a generally good thing – improves understanding – provides necessary support between generations
   ....

b most important general point to summarise why I hold my opinion – benefits individuals and communities
   ....

c lots more extended families than previously in my country, e.g. older generation, adult offspring stay at home
   ....

d economic pressures – hard to find jobs – child care – people living longer so more help needed
   ....

C Developing a clearly structured essay

Read the first part of this sample answer and fill in spaces 1–5 with expressions a–e.
Then fill in spaces 6–10 with a suitable word or phrase.

Nowadays in my own country there are more extended family households than previously. **1**............................ for grandparents to share a house with their children and grandchildren and for adult offspring to stay on in the family home rather than move away. **2**............................ for this trend internationally. One widely held view is that this may be due to economic factors. It is difficult for many young people to find well-paid jobs. **3**............................ house prices and rents are rising rapidly so it is more difficult to find anywhere cheap enough to live independently. **4**............................ for different generations to choose to live together is to provide support for each other. People are living longer and because of this they need more help from younger family members with practical matters such as cooking or health care. **5**............................, parents might need help from older relatives to look after their young children. In my view **6**............................ trend towards more extended family households is positive. Firstly, it is generally accepted that in cultures where older people live separately from the young there is often distrust between generations and I therefore feel that it is important for people of different ages to spend time together **7**............................ they can to have a better understanding of each other's attitudes. **8**............................, I take the view that it is a good thing for children to learn about the history of their area from older people **9**............................ it encourages them to take pride in the culture and identity of the place where they live. To conclude, I believe that having multi-generation households can benefit not only individuals but **10**............................ wider communities.	**a** For their part **b** Another possible reason **c** There are likely to be a number of reasons **d** It is now quite common **e** At the same time

The writer of the sample answer above has clearly stated that he/she believes having more extended families is a positive trend.

11 Below is the last part of an essay written by a candidate who holds the opposite view. The sentences have been mixed up. Reorder them to create a coherent paragraph. Remember to use the stage 1-4 structure.

a Although some extended families work out strategies to give each other mutual support, many of them simply end up quarrelling as they try to share limited space and resources.

b Older family members often try to tell younger ones what to do when they should be learning to make their own decisions.

c In my opinion, it is damaging for different age groups to live together.

d Firstly, in my experience many generations living together leads to friction.

e On balance, I do not think this is a positive trend.

f Secondly, I consider it a more natural thing for young adults to leave home and develop in their own direction, free from the constraints of the older generations.

g It is my view that communities that live closely together tend to lack dynamism and a capacity to grow and change.

Paragraphing

For Task 2 you <u>must</u> divide your text into paragraphs: you will receive a lower mark if you do not do this. There is no fixed number of paragraphs, but for a Task 2 text of 250 words, most good writers would have three or four.

There are no paragraphs marked in the sample answer above. Read through it again and decide where you would put in breaks. Use the symbol // to indicate where you would start a new paragraph.

Count the number of words in each of your paragraphs. Look back at the task on page 51 and think about the balance between the number of words in each stage.

Underline the first sentence of each paragraph and consider how it helps to guide the reader about what the section is about.

Useful language: academic vs colloquial language

1 Now read part of another answer to the task on page 51, one which is written in a colloquial rather than an academic style.

> Where I'm from more and more old people are living with their kids in big families – I'd say they do it more and more because it works out cheaper and it's nice to have people about to help if they need it.

TIP The word **colloquial** comes from the Latin word meaning **conversation**. We use colloquial language for talking informally to people we know. In the IELTS Academic Writing test you have to show that you can use consistently a more formal academic style, so it is important to recognise the distinct features of each style.

2 Find examples of the following features in the colloquial version.
   1 Simple vocabulary
   2 Dash – loose grammatical structures as if speaking, not writing in sentences
   3 Informal expressions, including phrasal verbs
   4 Repetition for emphasis
   5 Contractions
   6 Short explanations, no developed rationale

3 Now look back at the sample answer on page 53 and identify what makes it more suitable for an academic writing task. Find examples of each of these language features:
   1 More complex vocabulary
   2 Nouns instead of verbs
   3 Modal verbs
   4 Cautious language
   5 Complex grammatical structures
   6 Full forms, not contracted

Advice
Some people say you must not use first person pronouns (I, my) in formal academic writing. However, for IELTS Writing Task 2, you are encouraged to use them where appropriate, especially when discussing your own experience and opinions.

Useful language: impersonal structures

In academic writing it is useful to discuss opinions which are held by many people, without stating who these people are. The expression 'one widely held view' is an example of such an 'impersonal structure' in the sample answer on page 53.

1 Read through the rest of the text and find another example.

   Look at the following sentences and underline the impersonal structure in each one.
   a It is generally agreed that / Lots of people think aerobic exercise is beneficial.
   b People think that / One widely held opinion is that higher taxes lead to more equality.
   c Research suggests / I've heard that interactive learning is more effective.

Useful language: giving opinions

1 Look at these pairs of extracts from IELTS candidates' essays. Decide which ones use incorrect English and underline the part which should be corrected.
   1 A I strongly believe that this is a positive trend.
     B I am the opinion that this is a positive trend.
   2 A My feeling is that all theatres should be supported by the state.
     B I belief that all theatres should be supported by the state.
   3 A In my views it is crucial to pay females the same as males.
     B I feel it is crucial to pay females the same as males.

Useful language: cause and effect

There are two main ways of expressing cause and effect:
- **this** causes **that** (represented as A → B)
- **that** is caused by **this** (represented as B ← A)

1 Look at the following extracts from the sample answer on page 53. Underline the parts which refer to cause and effect and write them in the correct column of the table below. The first one has been done for you as an example.

   a … this <u>is due to</u> economic factors …
   b … rents are rising rapidly so it is more difficult to find anywhere cheap …
   c People are living longer and because of this they need more help …
   d … there is often distrust between generations and I therefore feel that it is important for people of different ages to spend time together …

A → B	B ← A
	is due to

Below are sentences containing other expressions for cause and effect.

2 Underline the cause and effect expressions and copy them into the correct column of the table.

   a High taxes result in a more equal society.
   b Social problems are often the result of deep inequality.
   c Owing to the resilience of the economy, it survived the financial crash.
   d Their success was a consequence of consistent effort.
   e Since young people do better in team work we assigned them to groups.

Writing Task 2

Useful language: adverbs of degree- cautious, qualifying language

One feature of good academic writing is the use of expressions which indicate caution. For example, 'on the whole' or 'generally' are qualifiers which show that a statement is mainly true, or true in most cases but not in all. They are useful because in academic writing you must not make sweeping generalised claims which you cannot prove.

1. Look at the following sentences and underline the adverbial word (or phrase) of degree. Think about why this has been used in each case.
    a People who have pets tend to have calmer temperaments.
    b In the main, cruise holidays are popular with older tourists.
    c The economy is usually strongly influenced by consumer confidence.

2. In b and c indicate another position where the adverb can go.

3. Choose a suitable adverb to qualify the following statements and indicate which different positions are acceptable.
    a Children attend school until the age of 16.
    b Non-fiction titles are more popular with males than females.
    c The weather in summer is drier than in winter.
    d People like more adventurous sports when they are younger.

Exam Practice Test 1 — Writing Task 2

Action plan for Writing Task 2
Before you write

1. Look at the task below and read the question carefully.
2. Underline important parts of the task.
3. Consider alternative language to express the points in the task.
4. Make notes on the task before you begin to write your essay. Your notes should cover the four essential stages described on page 52: an introduction, a discussion of the possible reasons for the trend, a discussion of whether this is a positive or negative development, concluding remarks which make your opinion clear.
5. Now write your essay.

TIP When you first read each IELTS tasks it is helpful to spend some time before you start writing to work out the key elements of the task. One way to do this is to try to paraphrase them, i.e. think of a different way to express the same point.

TIP If you have forgotten to use paragraphs, mark them using // in the correct places and write 'New Para' next to these marks in the margin.

TIP Although the quality of your English is the most important thing being assessed you will also need to show that you can discuss the topic in a relevant way. If you write about irrelevant points, your marks will be significantly reduced.

TIP Don't copy the question. Use your own words to introduce your essay. This is a fairly easy way to gain marks because assessors will be interested to see how well you can paraphrase in English.

After you write

6. Read through your answer carefully.
7. Check for:
   - **Overall structure** – have you included the four stages discussed on page 52?
   - **Paragraphing** – have you started a new paragraph for each main stage? Is there a clear signposting sentence, usually at the beginning of each paragraph, which guides the reader about what the section will include?
   - **Coherence** – have you linked your ideas together clearly?
   - **Style** – have you used appropriately formal language? Have you used appropriate cautious language?
   - **Grammar and spelling** – are your verb forms correct? Have you used capitals, apostrophes and full stops correctly?
   - **Your habitual errors** – what are these?

Advice
It is important to remember than in the IELTS writing exam it is your English and your ability to write a well-developed argument which is being assessed, not the quality of your ideas.

Writing Task 2

You should spend 40 minutes on this task.

Write on the following topic:

Many people nowadays spend a large part of their free time using a smartphone.

What do you think are the reasons for this?

Do you think this is a positive or negative development?

Give reasons for your answer and include any relevant examples from your own knowledge and experience.

Write at least 250 words.

Training Test 1 — Speaking Part 1

What is Speaking Part 1?
- a conversation with the examiner lasting 4–5 minutes about two or three everyday topics

Task information
You have to:
- answer questions about yourself, for example about your home, your studies or work, your free time, the things you like and dislike, etc.
- Give full answers – usually in one or two sentences.

What does it test?
- your ability to communicate opinions and information on everyday topics and common experiences or situations

TIP Try to think in English before you go into the test because this will help you get ready to answer the first questions.

Useful language: study or work
The examiner may start by asking you whether you work or you are a student. He or she will then ask you three questions about your job or your studies.

1 **Collect language to talk about the topic.**

   Study
   - What: Make sure you know the words for the subjects you are studying e.g. biology, business
   - Where: Make sure you know the words for the place you are studying e.g. technical college, high school
   - Why: Think of words for why you decided to study your subjects e.g. interesting, good career prospects, help in the family business
   - How: Think of words to describe what you like about your studies e.g. learning new things, discussing things with my classmates, understanding my subject better

   Work
   - What: Make sure you know the words for the job that you do e.g. sales manager, nurse
   - Where: Make sure you know the words for the place where you work e.g. car factory, children's hospital
   - Why: Think of words for why you decided to do this job e.g. to help people, to get a good salary, to work abroad
   - How: Think of words to describe how you feel about your work e.g. satisfying, varied, friendly colleagues

2 **Look at the examiner's questions about work / study on page 63 and answer them using the words and phrases you have collected.**

3 **Collect useful words and phrases to talk about spending time with friends and other topics e.g. hobbies, sports, holidays, languages.**

Useful language: extending your answers

If you answer a question like, 'Do you use computers a lot?' with, 'Yes, I do', the examiner will probably ask you to extend your answer by saying 'Why?' So, it is better to give a longer answer – one or two sentences.

1 Answer these questions and include a reason or an example.
   1 Do you use computers a lot?
   2 When did you first learn to use a computer?
   3 What's your favourite kind of film?
   4 How often do you go to the cinema?
   5 Do you like watching sport on television?
   6 Which new sport would you like to try?

2 It can help you to speak more fluently if you use linking words to join your ideas, rather than speaking in very short sentences. Use these words to join the short sentences below: *because, but, and, or, although, when, rather than, unless, as well as, while.*
   a I use a computer every day. I need it for my work. I like to keep in touch with friends on social media.
   b I learned to use a computer at school. I was six. We did some exercises on it. We enjoyed playing games on it.
   c I like watching action films. I don't like romantic films. Sometimes action films are too violent.
   d I'd like to go to the cinema more often. I have a lot of homework.
   e I don't like watching sport. I watch if there is an international football match.
   f I'd like to try ice-skating. I am scared of falling over.

3 Look at the questions about spending time with friends on page 63 and answer them. Remember to give reasons for your answers and use some of the linking words in Exercise 2.

Training Test 1 Speaking Part 2

What is Speaking Part 2?
- a talk lasting 2 minutes

Task information
You have to:
- read about a task that the examiner gives you.
- prepare for 1 minute to give a talk about the task.
- start speaking when the examiner tells you to start.
- stop speaking when the examiner tells you to stop.
- answer one or two questions after your talk.

What does it test?
- your ability to talk for a longer time
- your ability to organise what you say and speak fluently about a personal experience

Useful strategies: preparation time
One minute is a very short time, so it's important to use it well. The examiner will give you some paper and a pencil, so you can make notes if you want. Notes should be short and clear, so you can use them to help you speak.

1. Look at the task on page 63 and decide what item of clothing you want to talk about.

2. Now make a note for each of the four points of the task. Keep each note short – no more than a few words. Don't write in complete sentences. When you have finished, look at the sample notes in the key. Compare your notes with them and decide which would be easier to use.

   Change your notes if necessary.

3. Look at the task on page 63 again and use your notes to give a talk. Make sure you time yourself and try to speak for 2 minutes.

TIP It is important to choose something that will give you enough to talk about to fill 2 minutes.

TIP It is best to write any notes in English rather than in your own language.

TIP You should talk about all four points of the task, but you don't have to talk about them in the same order as the task. You may have more to say about one or two points than the others.

Useful language: clothes and fashion

1. Link the adjectives on the left with the items of clothing on the right by drawing lines between them. Some adjectives go with more than one item of clothing.

checked	flat	floral	full	high-heeled		cap	dress	jacket	pullover
patterned	plain	round-necked		short-sleeved		scarf	shirt	shoes	skirt
long	striped	three-piece	tight	V-necked		suit	trousers		

It is very easy to use simple words like 'good' or 'nice' too much when describing things. Try to use a variety of adjectives.

TIP Try to vary the language you use when you are giving a talk. This will help you to get a higher mark.

2 What other words can you use to:

a describe something in a positive way: good, nice, useful

....

b describe something in a negative way: bad, uncomfortable, expensive

....

c describe the way something feels: soft, rough

....

d describe the style of something: smart, old-fashioned

....

e describe the way something makes you feel: comfortable, sad

....

Useful language: giving a talk

1 It is important to structure your talk well. In particular, you should introduce the topic clearly. Here are some simple ways to start your talk.

I'm going to tell you about ...
What I want to talk about is ...
I've decided to tell you about ...

2 Now go back to the notes you made for the task 'My favourite item of clothing'. Give the talk again, but this time record it and time yourself. Try to use some of the language you collected in Exercises 1 and 2.

TIP You don't have to tell the truth in your talk. You can describe something that didn't happen if you find that easier. Just remember to talk about all the task points.

3 Listen to your talk and consider how to make it even better.
- Was there a clear introduction?
- Were all the four task points covered?
- Was the vocabulary varied?
- Were you speaking clearly – too fast or too slowly?
- Were there any grammar mistakes, e.g. 's' missing at the end of he / she verbs?
- Was the talk long enough?

4 In the next few days, try preparing and giving talks on the topics below.

Remember to write notes first and then record and time each talk.
- a plan you had to change, why you changed it and what happened
- a film you have seen several times and what you particularly liked about it
- a special meal you had with friends and why you remember it

Speaking Part 2   Training Test 1

Training Test 1 — Speaking Part 3

What is Speaking Part 3?
- a discussion of more general and abstract ideas related to the topic in Part 2 lasting 4–5 minutes

What does it test?
- your ability to use more formal and abstract language and discuss ideas in more depth

Task information

You have to:
- answer questions connected to the topic in Part 2, expressing your opinions and giving reasons for your views.
- answer 3–6 questions.

Useful language: expressing opinions

1 As in Part 2, it is important to use a range of language. It is very easy to introduce opinions by always saying 'I think'. Look at these other ways of introducing opinions.

> *Personally, I find that …*
> *In my opinion / view …*
> *It seems clear to me that …*
> *I (don't) agree with the idea that …*
> *I'd say that …*

2 Practise the expressions above when responding to these questions about stress.
  1 What are the best ways to reduce stress?
  2 Do you agree that people's lives are more stressful now than in the past?
  3 How easy is it to balance work and personal life in today's world?

Useful language: justifying opinions

When you give an opinion, the examiner may ask you to explain why you think that. He or she may also put forward the opposite view and ask for your comments.

Fill in the spaces in the sentences below with these words: *question, evidence, mean, reason, point*
  1 I see what you .... but in my view people are expected to work much harder nowadays.
  2 In my opinion, feeling happy at work is largely a .... of how supportive your colleagues are.
  3 The main .... of the students' campaign is that it costs too much to go to university now.
  4 The .... I believe that some courses are becoming too hard is the increasing number of students who drop out of college.
  5 There is a lot of .... now that proves people are under pressure.

TIP The examiner will record the Speaking test. This is for administrative reasons. Don't pay any attention to the recorder, just look at the examiner.

Exam Practice Test 1 — Speaking Parts 1-3

Speaking Part 1

The examiner will start by introducing him / herself and checking your identity. He or she will then ask you some questions about yourself.

Let's talk about what you do. Do you work or are you a student?

Work
- What's your job?
- Why did you choose this kind of work?
- What do you like most about your job?

Study
- What are you studying?
- Why did you choose this subject / these subjects?
- What do you like most about your studies?

> **TIP** The examiner will select either the questions about work or the ones about study depending on your answer to this question

The examiner will then ask you some questions about one or two other topics, for example:

Let's talk about spending time with friends.
1 When do you spend time with your friends?
2 Do you usually go out with friends or spend time with them at home?
3 Do you prefer to spend time with a large group of friends or just a few?
4 Did you do different things with your friends when you were younger?

> **TIP** Listen carefully to the questions. Questions 1-3 are about the present, while Question 4 is about the past.

Speaking Part 2

The examiner will give you a topic like the one below and some paper and a pencil.

The examiner will say:

I'm going to give you a topic and I'd like you to talk about it for one to two minutes. Before you talk, you'll have one minute to think about what you're going to say. You can make some notes if you wish.

[1 minute]

All right? Remember you have one to two minutes for this, so don't worry if I stop you. I'll tell you when the time is up. Can you start speaking now, please?

> **TIP** If you don't understand some words on the task, the examiner can say them in a simpler way for you. Just tell the examiner you don't understand. You won't lose marks for this.

> **TIP** Don't worry if you are still speaking when the examiner tells you to stop. It's better to speak right up to the 2-minute limit than to speak for 90 seconds.

> **Describe your favourite item of clothing**
> You should say:
>   what the item of clothing is
>   what it looks like
>   when and where you got this item of clothing
>   and explain why this is your favourite item of clothing.

> **TIP** The examiner will give marks across all three parts of the test, not a separate mark for each part.

The examiner may ask one or two rounding off questions when you have finished your talk, for example:
- Do you enjoy shopping for clothes?

Speaking Part 3

The examiner will ask some general questions which are connected to the topic in Part 2, for example:

We've been talking about your favourite item of clothing. I'd like to discuss with you one or two more general questions relating to this. First, let's consider different types of clothes.
- What kinds of clothes do young people like to wear in your country?

Let's talk about shopping habits now.
- Will people continue to shop in small shops and markets in the future?

Finally, let's talk about the fashion industry.
- What contribution does the fashion industry make to a country's economy and reputation?

Training Test 2 — Listening Part 1

Review
1. How many speakers will you hear?
2. Does each task in this part have the same number of questions?
3. What kind of information do you have to listen for in Part 1?
4. Do you have to write the exact words you hear?
5. Is spelling important in Part 1?

Now follow the Action plan reminder on page 65

Useful strategy: deciding what kind of information to write in the spaces

It is very important to look at the words around each space in the notes or form. These words will help you predict the type of information you are looking for.

1. Look at this set of notes. Underline the important information around each space. What does this tell you about the missing information? Try to predict possible answers. The first one has been done for you as an example.
   Write **ONE WORD ONLY** for each answer.

Accommodation at Sunnyside Holiday Park

Motel rooms
- $205; sleep 2 people
- all rooms have <u>a view of</u> the
  1 ....

Studios
- $155; sleep 4 people
- no kitchen but a kettle and
  2 ....
  for making drinks and snacks

Budget units
- $222; sleep 4 people
- kitchen with a fridge and
  3 ....
- need to bring your own
  4 ....

Other facilities
- laundry
- games room for all ages
- a **5** .... for guests under 12

Advice

Example: a view of
- *so, the answer must be something that is nice to look at*
- *possible answers: lake, sea, river, city, etc.*

🎧 2 Now listen and complete the information.
(11)

Useful vocabulary: accommodation registration forms

Look at the completed guest registration form. Complete the spaces using words from the box.

> Country
> Date and Place of Birth
> Date of Issue   Departure Date
> Expiry Date   Home Address
> Nationality   Postcode
> Room No.   Street
> Surname   Title

Guest Registration Form

1 .... Ms   **2** .... Rousseau   **First Name** Angelique

Arrival Date 6 April   **3** .... 8 April   **4** 1016

Credit Card   **Credit Card Number**   **5** 05.19
DigiCard   XXXX XXXX XXXX XXXX

Business Address [X]   **6** .... ✓   **City** Paris

7 ....   **8** 70115   **E-mail**
12 Rue de la Parc   a.rouss eau17@exposte.com

9 .... France   **Telephone** 01 83 77 29 54   **Passport Number**
                                                               224674429

10 ....   **11** .... French   **12** 7.9.2017
18.3.1999   Lyon

---

64   Training Test 2   Listening Part 1

Exam Practice Test 2 — Listening Part 1

Action plan reminder for *Table, note and form completion*
1. How do you know how many words to write?
2. Do you have time to look at the task before you hear the recording?
3. What can you learn from the words around the space?
4. How do you know the topic?

Questions 1–5

Complete the notes below.

Write **NO MORE THAN ONE WORD** for each answer.

New Apartment

Example   *Answer*
Landlady's Name: Mary Jones

General
- partly furnished
- no **1** .... are allowed

Kitchen
- nice and big
- there is a new **2** ....

Lounge
- some **3** .... will be built soon

Bedroom
- good clothes storage
- need to bring a **4** ....

Bathroom
- only a shower
- the water is heated by **5** ....

TIP Not every piece of information in the notes / form / table contains a space. This helps you follow the conversation.

TIP Most missing information is facts about the topic, so the answers are usually nouns (or dates, names, numbers, etc.).

TIP Don't just write down the first word you hear that fits the space because there may be distractors. Keep listening until you hear the correct information.

TIP All the answers are words from the text. Don't write down any word that isn't in the text.

Advice

1 Think of synonyms for **allowed**.

2 The word **new** is important here – listen for distraction.

3 This must be something that can be **built** – not just something that will happen in the future.

Questions 6–10

Complete the form below.

Write **ONE WORD AND / OR A NUMBER** for each answer.

Tenancy Form

Tenant details
- Full name: Andrew **6** ....
- Best contact: **7** andrew171@ .... .com
- Driver's licence: **8** ....

Tenancy details
- Moving-in date: **9** ....
- Rent per week: $315
- **Bond paid**: 10 $ ....

Advice

6 Look out for letters that are easily confused, such as **m** and **n**, **b** and **t**, etc.

8 Some **numbers** are actually a mixture of letters and numbers!

TIP Be careful not to write down any information that is already given in the form / notes / table, e.g. **$** or **a** or **the**, etc.

TIP Use the subheadings in the form / notes / table to help you follow the conversation and predict what you will hear next.

TIP Make sure your answer fits the grammar around the space, e.g. is the missing word singular or plural?

Training Test 2 — Listening Part 2

Review
1 How many speakers will you hear in this part?
2 How many tasks are there usually?
3 Does each task have the same number of questions?
4 What is the speaker's purpose in this part?

Now follow the Action plan reminder on page 68

Useful vocabulary: entertainment

1 Which answer (**A, B or C**) best fits each space?

 1 The whole family enjoyed seeing the acrobats and clowns when the .... came to town.
   A zoo   **B** amusement park   **C** circus

 2 In my view, Paul Fernley is one of the finest .... of his generation. He's the star of every movie he appears in, even if it's only a minor part.
   A directors   **B** actors   **C** cameramen

 3 It was a great show and I got sore hands from .... so much!
   A booing   **B** clapping   **C** cheering

 4 Mozart was an extraordinary .... and people still love listening to the music he wrote more than 200 years after his death.
   A composer   **B** conductor   **C** choreographer

 5 This weekend I'm going to see the exhibition of dinosaur fossils that's opening at the ....
   A theatre   **B** art gallery   **C** museum

 6 On Friday evening I was planning to .... but in the end I was so tired I stayed at home.
   A go out   **B** play up   **C** drop off

Task information: *Matching tasks*

You may have to match information in a box with words that you hear.
Look at this example about entertainment events.

A enjoyable for children
B no cost is involved
C requires fine weather

 1 If a speaker said the following, would it match option **A**, **B** or **C**?

   '… and this event will be really popular with those aged under 10.'

 2 You will hear five speakers making comments about a variety of entertainment events. Listen and match what each speaker says to one of the options (**A, B or C**) in the box.

Speaker 1: ....
Speaker 2: ....
Speaker 3: ....
Speaker 4: ....
Speaker 5: ....

Exam Practice Test 2 — Listening Part 2

Action plan reminder for *3-option multiple-choice*
1. What should you do before you listen?
2. How do you know the answer to the next question is coming?
3. Will the words in the options (A, B and C) be the same as the words in the recording?
4. What should you do when you hear an answer?

TIP The main speaker may be introduced by another speaker.

TIP The questions follow the order of information in the recording.

Questions 11–15.

Choose the correct letter, A, B or C.

11 What is new about the Writers' Festival this year?
- A more international guests
- B extra time for questions
- C additional locations for events

12 Tickets for the Wearable Art event
- A are selling out quickly.
- B have been reduced in price.
- C must be booked in advance.

13 Ocean Times at Bright's Beach is
- A a sporting competition for adults.
- B an educational event for all ages.
- C a play day for young children.

14 People going to the Artscape Exhibition
- A should wear appropriate clothing.
- B must keep to the proper path.
- C need to arrive at a certain time.

15 Tours of the Civil Theatre
- A do not happen often.
- B have never happened before.
- C may happen more regularly in future.

Advice

11 Listen for what is new about this year's festival and watch out for distractors.

13 Listen for the type of event and the type of person it will appeal to.

14 Listen for the advice the speaker gives.

15 Watch out for distractors!

TIP You may hear information in the recording that relates to all three options (**A**, **B** and **C**) but some of this is distraction.

TIP The information in the options (**A**, **B** and **C**) does not necessarily follow the order of information in the recording.

Action plan for *Matching tasks*

1. Read the instructions carefully. In some *matching tasks* you use each letter in the box more than once. In other *matching tasks* there are more options in the box and you use each letter once only.
2. Read the options in the box. Think about words you might hear that have a similar meaning.
3. Look at the names of the people, places, events, etc. that you need to match to the options.
4. Match the people, etc. with the information in the box.
5. Check your answers and then transfer them to the answer sheet at the end of the recording. Make sure you transfer the answers for both tasks!

TIP At the end of the first task there is a pause in the recording. Use this time to read the questions for the next task.

Questions 16–20

What comment does the speaker make about each of the following events?

Write the correct letter, **A**, **B** or **C**, next to questions 16–20.

You may use any letter more than once.

Comments

A the location has changed
B transport will be a problem
C the event might be crowded

Events

16 Night Market ....
17 Buskers Festival ....
18 Stand Up for Kids ....
19 Sunday Unplugged ....
20 Ignite Dance Finals ....

Advice

16 Watch out for words or phrases that can have different meanings.
17 Listen for the words that the speaker stresses.
18 What advice does the speaker give?

TIP The words in the options (**A**, **B** and **C**) will not be the same as the words in the recording. Listen for synonyms and paraphrase.

Listening Part 2 — Exam Practice Test 2

Training Test 2 — Listening Part 3

Review
1. How many speakers are there?
2. What is the subject of the discussion?
3. How many tasks are there?
4. What does Part 3 test?

Now follow the Action plan reminder on pages 71-2

Useful strategy: identifying opinions

You may need to identify the opinions of speakers, rather than facts about a topic.

1. Look at the pairs of sentences below. For each pair, identify which sentence is a fact and which is an opinion.
   1. a. The research sample was too small.
      b. Twenty-five research subjects took part in the experiment.
   2. a. It's been estimated that about 72% of Australian adults do not speak a second language.
      b. More Australian adults should learn to speak a language other than English.
   3. a. I didn't start learning a second language until I was an adult, when I did a course at night school for three hours a week.
      b. More research should be conducted into the experiences of people who start learning a second language as adults.
   4. a. Learners of English as a second language need a vocabulary of approximately 4,000 to 10,000 words.
      b. The fourth edition of the *Cambridge Advanced Learner's Dictionary* contains over 140,000 words, phrases, meanings and examples, plus hundreds of pictures and illustrations.
   5. a. Linguist Dr Margot McCloud claims that an adult can achieve basic fluency in a second language in three months, based on 10 hours of work per day.
      b. Trying to estimate how long it will take an adult to learn a second language is a mistake because there are so many variables involved.

Useful strategy: identifying the speaker's attitude

1. Listen to the following excerpts. In each case, decide which option, A or B, best describes the speaker's attitude.
   1. A. amused by the behaviour of other class members
      B. disappointed by the actions of other class members
   2. A. impressed he received the test results so quickly
      B. shocked when he received his test results
   3. A. surprised that vocabulary was considered so important
      B. confused about why vocabulary wasn't considered more important

Exam Practice Test 2 — Listening Part 3

Action plan reminder for *5-option multiple-choice*
1. How do you know what type of information you are listening for?
2. Are the words used in the questions the same as the words in the conversation?
3. Are the two answers (options **A–E**) in the same order in the conversation?

TIP Don't use your own knowledge of a subject. Listen to what the students say.

TIP Sometimes you are listening for the speakers' opinions, not facts about the topic.

Questions 21–22

*Choose **TWO** letters, **A–E**.*

What **TWO** problems do the students identify with 'learning videos'?
- **A** Babies lose interest too quickly.
- **B** Babies need to explore things.
- **C** Babies want to be with other babies.
- **D** Babies' eyes may be damaged.
- **E** Babies should have contact with adults.

Advice
21 and **22** Focus on problems identified by both students.
23 and **24** Focus on Maia's attitude towards the research.

Questions 23–24

*Choose **TWO** letters, **A–E**.*

When discussing the 'present research', Maia is surprised that
- **A** ordinary people have altered their habits.
- **B** the findings are very detailed.
- **C** most babies behave the same way.
- **D** boys and girls like different toys.
- **E** the methodology has been criticised.

TIP Remember to write **TWO** letters on the answer sheet.

Questions 25–26

*Choose **TWO** letters, **A–E**.*

What impresses the students about the bilingual experiment in Spain?
- **A** the long-term effects of the lessons
- **B** the large number of research subjects
- **C** the fact that the children enjoyed themselves
- **D** the fact that teachers had the same training
- **E** the response of schools to the findings

Action plan reminder for *Matching tasks*

1. Can you write each letter in the box more than once?
2. Are you given time to read the questions?
3. Are the words in the box the same as the words in the recording?
4. Are the words in the questions (e.g. 27–30) the same as the recording?

TIP The questions (**27–30**) follow the order of information in the recording.

TIP The options (**A–F**) are in random order.

Questions 27–30

What was the finding of each of the following research studies?

Choose **FOUR** answers from the box and write the correct letter (**A–F**) next to **Questions 27–30**.

Findings

A Babies understand cause and effect.
B Babies like physical exercise.
C Babies like their actions to be copied.
D Babies are excited by surprises.
E Babies recognise basic grammar.
F Babies like to help other people.

Advice

27 Listen to the end of Maia's turn before selecting the answer.

28 Maia asks a question. Listen carefully to Daniel's reply.

29 Pay particular attention to the use of paraphrase.

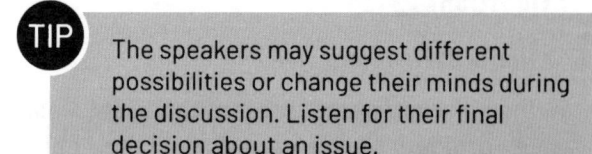

TIP The speakers may suggest different possibilities or change their minds during the discussion. Listen for their final decision about an issue.

TIP There may be two or three options that you do not need to use.

Research studies

27 Dr Pritchard's study ....
28 The three-year-olds study ....
29 Professor Michelson's study ....
30 The United States study ....

Training Test 2 — Listening Part 4

Review
1. How many speakers will you hear?
2. What kind of topic might you hear?
3. How many questions do you have to answer?
4. How many tasks are there?

Now follow the Action plan reminder on page 74

Useful strategy: following the speaker

When completing notes (or a table, flow-chart, form, etc.) it is important to listen for signposting language that shows you how the text is organised. This helps you follow the speaker and locate each answer.

Here are three common types of signposting language:
- A Moving to the next stage of a lecture
- B Giving an example
- C Substitution words referring to something already mentioned

1 Read these expressions and mark each one A, B or C to show what kind of signposting language it could be. For some expressions, you can use more than one letter.

1 Then, there's also the issue of …	6 The first one concerns …	11 One that stood out for me was …
2 It didn't happen then because …	7 This can be exemplified by the fact that …	12 Another aspect worth noting is …
3 By way of illustration …	8 She had some difficulties there, however, because …	13 The research attracted some criticisms as well, including …
4 The reason for this was …	9 He achieved some notable successes, such as …	14 That experiment was a success …
5 In terms of the results, the researchers found that …	10 The next thing I want to consider is …	15 Now I'd like to discuss some reasons why …

Useful strategy: editing your work

1 Look at the notes below. This candidate has essentially understood the lecture and located the correct information to fill each space. However, the candidate has made some errors recording the answers. Find the errors and correct them. Not all the notes are incorrect.

Complete the notes below.

Write **ONE WORD ONLY** for each answer.

The Engineer Isambard Kingdom Brunel, 1806–1859

Early life
- aged 8, Isambard had a detailed knowledge of **1** *geometry*
- he went to **2** *university* in France
- aged 20 he helped his father build a **3** *a tunnel* near London
- they used a new technique to make the project more **4** *safety*

Great Western Railway
- he designed every detail including **5** *station*, lamp posts and carriages
- his focus was speed and **6** *comfort* for passengers
- he was criticised for using wide tracks which were **7** *too expensive*

Other
- the Clifton Suspension Bridge is suspended between two stone **8** *tower*
- in 1843 he built the SS *Great Britain*, then the largest ship made of **9** *metal*
- he designed a type of mobile **10** *hospitals*

Exam Practice Test 2 — Listening Part 4

Action plan reminder for *Note completion*

1. How do you know how many words to write?
2. How do you know what the lecture will be about?
3. What is the best way to follow the recording?
4. How do you know what information to listen for?

Questions 31–40

Complete the notes.

*Write **ONE WORD ONLY** for each answer.*

The Engineer Sarah Guppy, 1770–1852

Background
- women were active in many areas of 19th-century British society, e.g. Jane Harrison was the first female **31** _____
- by the end of the century there were 140 female dentists and 212 **32** _____, as well as many musicians and actors

Sarah Guppy
- was born in Birmingham and moved to Bristol with her husband
- designed bridges that could survive **33** _____
- built **34** _____ of the Clifton Suspension Bridge
- was a significant **35** _____ in the Clifton Suspension Bridge together with her husband
- designed a 'barnacle buster' that allowed **36** _____ to go faster
- helped stop **37** _____ near railway lines
- built an amusing machine for making different parts of **38** _____ at the same time
- designed an early type of **39** _____ equipment

Conclusions
- other women worked as engineers, e.g. Ada Lovelace and Hertha Marks Ayrton
- it was not until 1906 that a woman **40** _____ in engineering

TIP Remember to use the locating words in each note to help you follow the information in the recording (e.g. names, places, dates, nouns, etc.).

TIP Always edit your own answers carefully. Check for simple mistakes such as spelling, plurals, etc.

TIP If the instructions say **ONE WORD ONLY**, don't write two words. Your answer will be incorrect.

Advice

31 What might her professional role have been?

32 The jobs listed in the question are in a different order in the recording.

33 Listen for something that could cause a bridge to fall down.

35 This must be an activity she did jointly with her husband.

36 There are clear locating words here. Also, listen for a synonym for **faster**.

37 Listen for something negative that could damage railway lines if not stopped.

Training Test 2 — Reading Passage 1

Review

1 Does each task have the same number of questions?
2 Are the questions in the same order as the information you need in the text?
3 Can you use your own general knowledge or must the answer come from the text?
4 What are the different tasks you might have to do for this passage?

Now follow the Action plan reminder on page 76

Useful strategies: *True / False / Not given*

In extracts A–F decide if there is *enough* information to make the statements 1 – 6 TRUE / FALSE or NOT GIVEN. (Remember a FALSE statement must clearly *disagree with* or say the *opposite* thing to the information in the extract.)

A Babies begin to make their first sounds of laughter at around four months but not because something seems humorous to them. Instead, laughter is a non-verbal means of communication. And so it is for adults, too.

1 Babies and adults sometimes find the same kind of things funny. **FALSE / NOT GIVEN**

Strategy: Finding examples. Look for a description of a situation or an example of a joke or story that people might find amusing.

B In meal preparation, some people insist on using only unprocessed grey salt, which they believe will do you more good than the factory-refined white salt found on supermarket shelves. In fact, this processed kind would make more sense in nutritional terms, since it contains iodine, a vital element for our physical well-being.

2 Processed salt sold by supermarkets is a healthier product than the unprocessed kind. **TRUE / NOT GIVEN**

*Strategy: Identifying important adjectives. Think about how **healthier** might be paraphrased in the text.*

C When the Greeks and Romans began importing blue dye in 400 BC, it came in small, hard blocks, which they believed was a mineral. It took several centuries before they discovered the dye's true source, an Indian plant.

3 In 400 BC the Greeks and Romans thought the blue dye was made from an Indian plant. **FALSE / NOT GIVEN**

*Strategy: Recognising when information is complete or incomplete. Look at the text after **400 BC**. Does the writer talk about the Greek and Roman beliefs about the way that blue dye was made? If not, choose NOT GIVEN. Or does the writer explain the Greek and Roman beliefs? If so, what did they believe?*

D The team have discovered that snowfall in Antarctica has increased by 10 per cent over the last 200 years. While this may suggest to some people that climate change is not as bad as we feared, team leader Erica Wright maintains the snowfall is a consequence of global warming. In other words, the snowfall is not the positive sign we might hope for.

4 Erica Wright believes that human activity is mainly responsible for climate change. **TRUE / NOT GIVEN**

*Strategy: Identifying cause and consequence. Look for examples of **human activity** that might cause climate change, or phrases such as **In Erica's opinion, people have contributed to/are the cause of/are to blame for this problem**.*

E Around 35,000 children aged between 4 and 15 had one or more teeth removed because of infection in 2017, according to the latest survey. That figure is likely to climb.

5 Children in their teens suffer from worse tooth decay than younger children. **TRUE / NOT GIVEN**

*Strategy: Finding language of comparison. Look for phrases such as **as bad as**, **compared with**, **less/more**.*

F What can be done about low numbers of shellfish? According to David Lemi, too much attention has been on the quantity of shellfish harvested. Instead, he says, we should be challenging harvesting that destroys their habitat.

6 David Lemi wants shellfish collection to be restricted to areas of the ocean. **FALSE / NOT GIVEN**

*Strategy: Identifying important verbs. If you can find another word for **restricted** in the text, choose False.*

New Zealand's early crafts and traditions

The first groups of people to discover New Zealand came from Polynesia. Exactly when these explorers arrived has often been a matter of debate, but today the general understanding is that it was during the 13th century that their canoes eventually landed on New Zealand's shores. In some ways the new country must have seemed like an ideal place to settle: the land was fertile, and thick forests provided firewood, shelter and building materials. Still, life would have been challenging for the different Polynesian tribes, who had to adapt to a new environment. The tribes only began to refer to themselves as *Māori*, meaning 'ordinary people', when Europeans in search of new opportunities began arriving in the 18th century. To the Maori, of course, the European settlers and sailors were not 'ordinary', but very strange.

It was not only a knowledge of canoe-building and navigation that the Polynesians brought to New Zealand. They were also skilled craftsmen. There is archaeological evidence that the tools they produced were of high quality and would have enabled tribes to plant and harvest crops. Craftsmen were also occupied with making weapons such as knives and axes, which were used for both construction and fighting. Interestingly, some crafts that had once been popular in Polynesian islands were no longer done in New Zealand, although researchers are unsure why. Pottery is an example of this, despite the fact that the clay needed to make pots and bowls could easily be found in the new country.

The Maori word *whakairo* can be translated as 'decorative work' – this can refer to bone, wood and greenstone carving. Although Maori carvers were influenced by their Polynesian heritage, they developed their own style, including the curved patterns and spirals inspired by New Zealand plants. The same term can also apply to weaving; the crafting of, for example, woven baskets and mats all required knowledge and skill. Carving greenstone, or *pounamu* as it is called in Maori, was a long process, requiring great patience. Further, because of this mineral's rarity, any greenstone object, such as a piece of jewellery or cutting blade, was a prized possession. For that reason, it was the few people of high status rather than low-ranking members of a tribe who would possess such objects.

As New Zealand had no native mammals except for bats, dolphins and whales, Maori largely had to depend on plants to provide material for their clothing, including their cloaks. Weavers experimented with the inner bark of the *houhere*, the lacebark tree, but found it unsuitable. But the dried-out leaves and fibres of the flax plant provided a solution. Once a cloak had been woven from flax, it could be decorated. Borders might be dyed black or red, for example. In the case of superior ones made for chiefs or the more important members of a tribe, feathers from kiwi, pigeons or other native birds might be attached. All flax cloaks were rectangular in shape, so had no sleeves, and neither was a hood a feature of this garment. Short cloaks were fastened around a person's neck, and came only to the waist. Pins made of bone, wood or greenstone allowed longer cloaks to be secured at the shoulder; these were a type that were often used for ceremonial occasions. Of course, the construction of the cloaks was influenced by the plant material available to Maori weavers. This meant that cloaks were loose-fitting, and while they protected wearers from New Zealand's strong sunshine, they were not useful during the winter months. A cloak made from fur or wool could provide insulation from the cold, but not so a cloak made of flax.

The warriors of a tribe required a different kind of cloak to help protect them. To create these special cloaks, the tough fibres of the mountain cabbage tree were used instead. It is not clear to researchers what the entire process involved, but they believe the fibres were left to soak in water over a period of time in order to soften them and make them easier to weave together. Later, once the whole cloak had been constructed, it would be dyed black. To do this, Maori weavers covered it in a special kind of mud they had collected from riverbeds. This was rich in iron due to New Zealand's volcanic landscape. The particular advantage of these cloaks was that the tough cabbage tree fibres they were woven from could reduce the impact of spear tips during a fight with enemy tribes. It is fortunate that some cloaks from the 1800s still survive and can provide us with further insight into the materials and construction techniques that Maori craftsmen used.

Questions 1–6

Do the following statements agree with the information given in Reading Passage 1?

In boxes 1–6 on your answer sheet, write

TRUE	if the statement agrees with the information
FALSE	if the statement contradicts the information
NOT GIVEN	if there is no information on this

1. It is now widely thought that humans reached New Zealand in the 13th century.
2. The first Europeans to come to New Zealand were keen to trade with Maori.
3. Members of Maori tribes were responsible for either tool- or weapon-making.
4. A craft that the Maori once practised in New Zealand was making pottery.
5. Weaving baskets and mats was seen as a form of decorative work by the Maori.
6. It used to be common for everyone in a Maori tribe to wear greenstone jewellery.

Advice

1 Find the reference to the 13th century and underline any words in the first two sentences which are used instead of **humans**. Look for a phrase which means something similar or opposite to **widely thought**.

2 Find the locating word **Europeans**. Can you see any phrases that mean something similar to **trade** or examples of things that might be traded?

3 Look for the locating words **tools** and **weapons**. Does this part of the text mainly focus on the uses of tools or weapons, or on the people who made them?

4 Where does it talk about pottery in the passage? What does **this** refer to in **Pottery is an example of this**?

5 Read the explanation about **decorative work** in the third paragraph. Does it include information only on carving, or does it include weaving too?

6 Locate **jewellery** in the third paragraph. Is there any information in this part of the passage that shows what kind of Maori wore jewellery?

Task information: *Table, Note, Flow-chart completion, Diagram labelling*

When completing a table, a set of notes, a flow-chart or a diagram, it is important to:
- read and follow the instructions at the top of the task.
- predict what kind of word might fit the space, e.g. a noun or adjective, plural or singular.
- check that the notes etc. make sense after you add the word/words that you think are the answers.
- spell the word / words correctly on your answer sheet.

1 Read the rubric below. Then look at a student's answers for questions 1–6 and think about why each answer must be wrong.

Questions 1–6

Complete the notes below.

Choose **ONE WORD ONLY** from the passage for each answer.

1. Maori decorated their kites with ......*shell*...... as these made a loud rattling noise.
2. A special T-shaped kite was often flown in a ......*compitition*...... .
3. People sometimes sent a kite up as a ......*warn*...... when enemies approached.
4. Maori sometimes created ......*kites*...... for the first time they flew their kites.
5. Before Europeans arrived, kites were flown by ......*children*...... as well as young members of a tribe.
6. Kites were often designed to look like birds and the ......*human faces*...... of people.

2 Now match the students' answers with an explanation of why they are wrong.

A This answer doesn't make sense because the same word is already in the notes.

B The student hasn't copied the word accurately, so the spelling is wrong.

C The answer suggests that the student didn't read the rubric carefully. The student won't get a mark for this answer, even though one of the words is correct.

D The student didn't notice that their answer means the same thing as the last part of the question. The student should have chosen an answer that meant something *different*, such as 'adults'.

E The answer needs to be plural. The student should have underlined the word 'these'.

F The answer shows that the student was probably looking at the right part of the text. However, the student needed to find a noun, such as 'signal' or 'message', because a verb doesn't fit in the space.

TIP Look at the subheadings in the table. These give you a general idea of where the answers are located in the final two paragraphs.

TIP Use your general knowledge to help you predict what kind of information is required for each space. This may save you time locating the real answers in the passage.

Questions 7–13

Complete the table below.

Choose **NO MORE THAN TWO WORDS** from the passage for each answer.

Write your answers in boxes 7–13 on your answer sheet.

	Maori cloaks	
	flax cloaks	**warrior cloaks**
methods of construction	Maori made flax cloaks by – weaving leaves and fibres – sometimes adding **7** .... to the better cloaks	Weavers had to use **11** .... to make cabbage tree fibres less stiff
appearance	Flax cloaks were – rectangular in shape – designed without a **8** .... – tied at either the wearer's neck or their **9**	Mud containing **12** .... was used to make the cloaks look black
good / bad points	Flax cloaks offered no **10** .... during winter	**13** .... could not easily go through the cloak's tough fibres

Advice

7 Look for paraphrases of **adding** and **better**.

8 What shape might a cloak have?

9 Where might a person tie a cloak around their body?

10 For what reasons do people usually wear cloaks? Find one of these in the fourth paragraph.

11 Look for a process that describes how the leaves of cabbage trees are made less tough.

12 You need a substance that might be found inside mud.

13 Find something that the tough fibres of a cloak might stop. Because there is no article (a/an), you will need to find an uncountable noun or a plural form.

Reading Passage 1

Training Test 2 — Reading Passage 2

Review

1. Is Passage 2 based around opinion and discussion, or is it more factual and descriptive?
2. Does Passage 2 contain only the views of the writer?
3. How many tasks did you do for Passage 2, Test 1? What did you have to do for each task?
4. How long should you spend on this section?

In Test 2, you will focus on three other tasks that you may be required to do for Passage 2:

Matching information, *Sentence completion* and *5-option multiple-choice*.

Task information: *Matching information*

A *Matching information* task is different from a *Matching headings* task because:
- the information you are looking for is only in *part* of a paragraph.
- a paragraph can be chosen more than once.
- not all paragraphs will be needed as answers.
- the questions start with a phrase showing the type of information that must be located.

1 Look at phrases 1–5 showing the type of information you might need to locate. Match them with extracts A–E. Some phrases have been underlined to help you.

1	**a contrast between** the results of …	A	From his experiment, Professor Kelly has concluded that there is likely to be a link between diet and dementia. However, Australian neurologist Satoshi Ohsumi <u>has pointed out a possible problem with</u> the experiment.
2	**a warning about** the outcome of …	B	In Andrevski's opinion, the organisation <u>was wrong to</u> cut back on health and safety training for new employees. 'They <u>should not have done this</u> without consulting managers,' he says.
3	**a reason why** one group …	C	If the government does not take action soon, it <u>seems almost certain</u> that plastic pollution will only get worse.
4	**a challenge to** a theory about …	D	<u>Whereas</u> some patients who took part in the study reported a definite improvement in mobility, others said the exercises made no difference at all.
5	**a criticism of** one company's approach …	E	Teens are less able to control emotions <u>because</u> their pre-frontal cortex has not yet developed.

Sleep should be prescribed: what those late nights out could be costing you

Leading neuroscientist Matthew Walker on why sleep deprivation is bad for us – and what you can do about it

A Matthew Walker dreads the question 'What do you do?' On an aeroplane it usually means that while everyone else watches movies, he will find himself giving a talk for the benefit of passengers and crew alike. To be specific, Walker is the director of the Center for Human Sleep Science at the University of California. No wonder people long for his advice. As the line between work and leisure grows more blurred, rare is the person who *doesn't* worry about their sleep. Indeed, it's Walker's conviction that we are in the midst of a 'catastrophic sleep-loss epidemic'. He has now written *Why We Sleep*, the idea being that once people know of the powerful links between sleep loss and poor health, they will try harder to get the recommended eight hours a night. Sleep deprivation constitutes anything less than seven. 'No one is doing anything about it but things have to change. But when did you ever see a national health service poster urging sleep on people? When did a doctor prescribe, not sleeping pills, but sleep itself? It needs to be prioritised.'

B Why are we so sleep-deprived in this century? In 1942, less than 8% of the population was trying to survive on six hours or less sleep a night; in 2017, almost one in two people is. Some reasons are obvious, but Walker believes, too, that in the developed world sleep is strongly associated with weakness. 'We want to seem busy, and one way we express that is by proclaiming how little sleep we're getting. When I give lectures, people wait behind until there is no one around and then tell me quietly: "I seem to be one of those people who need eight or nine hours' sleep." It's embarrassing to say it in public.'

C Walker has found clear evidence that without sleep, there is low energy and disease, and with sleep, there is vitality and health. More than 20 studies all report the same relationship: the shorter your sleep, the shorter your life. For example, adults aged 45 years or older who sleep less than six hours a night are 200% more likely to have a heart attack, as compared with those sleeping seven or eight. This is because even one night of sleep reduction will affect a person's heart and significantly increase their blood pressure as a result. Walker also points out that when your sleep becomes short, you are susceptible to weight gain. Among the reasons for this are the fact that inadequate sleep increases levels of the hunger-signalling hormone, ghrelin. 'I'm not going to say that the obesity crisis is caused by the sleep-loss epidemic alone,' says Walker. 'However, processed food and sedentary lifestyles do not adequately explain its rise. It's now clear that sleep is that third ingredient.'

D Sleep also has a powerful effect on the immune system, which is why, when we have flu, our first instinct is to go to bed. If you are tired, you are more likely to get sick. The well-rested also respond better to the flu vaccine so this is something people should bear in mind before visiting their doctors. Walker's book also includes a long section on dreams. Here he details the various ways in which deep sleep – the part when we begin to dream – helps us deal with our emotional experiences. He points to how important deep sleep is to young children. If they don't get enough, managing aggressive behaviour becomes harder and harder. Does Walker take his own advice when it comes to sleep? 'Yes. I give myself a non-negotiable eight-hour sleep opportunity every night, and I keep very regular hours. I take my sleep incredibly seriously because I have seen the evidence.'

E Sleep research shows that we sleep in 90-minute cycles, and it's only towards the end of each that we go into deep sleep. Each cycle comprises of NREM sleep (non-rapid eye movement sleep), followed by REM (rapid eye movement) sleep. 'During NREM sleep ... your body settles into this lovely low state of energy,' Walker explains. 'REM sleep, on the other hand is ... an incredibly active brain state. Your heart and nervous system go through spurts of activity.' Because we need four or five of these cycles to stay healthy, it's important for people to break bad sleep habits. For example, they should not be regularly working late into the night as this affects cognitive functioning. Depending on sleeping pills is also not a good idea, as it can have a damaging effect on memory.

F So what can individuals do to ensure they get the right amount of sleep? Firstly, we could think about getting ready for sleep in the same way we prepare for the end of a workout – say, on a spin bike. 'People use alarms to wake up,' Walker says. 'So why don't we have a bedtime alarm to tell us we've got half an hour, that we should start cycling down?' Companies should think about rewarding sleep. Productivity will rise and motivation will be improved. We can also systematically measure our sleep by using personal tracking devices, Walker says, and points out that some far-sighted companies in the US already give employees time off if they get enough of it. While some researchers recommend banning digital devices from the bedroom because of their effect on the sleep-inducing hormone melatonin, Walker believes that technology will eventually be an aid to sleep, as it helps us discover more about the way we function.

Questions 14–18

Reading Passage 2 has six paragraphs, **A–F**.

Which paragraph contains the following information?

Write the correct letter, **A–F**, in boxes 14–18 on your answer sheet.

NB You may use any letter more than once.

14 a comparison between two different types of sleep that people experience
15 an explanation for some people not wanting to admit the amount of sleep they require
16 examples of different behaviours that have a negative impact on mental performance
17 a suggestion that medical professionals are not taking the right approach
18 a reference to changing trends in the average amount of sleep people get

Task information: *Sentence completion*

Sentence completion is similar to Passage 2 *Summary completion* because:
- the instructions will tell you how many words or numbers you can write.
- the information you need may be in one paragraph or spread over a longer part of the passage.
- the information will be in the same order as the sentences you need to complete.
- the locating words in the sentences will help find the right place in the passage.

1   Read through questions 19–22. Choose the underlined phrase, A or B, that is more likely to help you locate the information you need.

Questions 19–22

Complete the sentences below.

Choose **NO MORE THAN TWO WORDS** from the passage for each answer.

Write your answers in boxes 19–22 on your answer sheet.

19 Over 20 studies (A) have shown a person's .... goes up (B) when they are sleep deprived.
20 Insufficient sleep (A) is one of three factors (B) which explain the ....
21 People who are given the .... by doctors (A) find it more effective if they sleep properly (B).
22 Walker has described (A) how a lack of deep sleep is linked to .... in young children (B).

2   Now answer questions 19–22.

Advice

14 Scan the text for a paragraph containing a scientific explanation of what happens when people sleep. Check for words such as **whereas**, **on the other hand**, **while**.

15 A number of paragraphs mention **people** – but which paragraph specifically says they don't like talking about the amount of sleep they actually need?

16 How might **mental performance** be paraphrased in the text? Look for things people might do that have a harmful effect on this.

17 How might **medical professionals** be paraphrased? Are you looking for a positive comment about them, or a negative one?

18 When people talk about trends, what kind of language do you expect to see? Scan the text to find a paragraph with examples of this language.

Advice

19/20 studies is the locating phrase, but the information you need may not be in the same sentence. Continue reading until you find something that collocates with **go up**.

20 Another way to say **factor** is **reason** or **cause**. Scan for a reference to three different causes of a particular problem mentioned in the text.

21 Scan the text for a reference to doctors. Look for something in that paragraph that a doctor would give to a patient.

22 Only one paragraph mentions young children specifically. What effect does a lack of deep sleep have on them?

TIP The instructions explain that one or two words are allowed, but no more than two. Write two words if both are necessary to make sense.

TIP The locating phrase **20 studies** in question 19 shows you where to start looking for information. The information you need for questions 20–22 will come after this.

Task information: *5-option multiple-choice*

A *5-option multiple-choice* task requires you to:
- choose two correct options from a set of five.
- look for information contained in one paragraph or spread over a longer part of the passage.

You should:
- read the instructions carefully so you know what specific information to look for.
- check if a context-setting statement is included in the instructions, as this may tell you which part of the passage to look at.
- underline words and phrases in the options that might be paraphrased in the passage.

1 Read the example instructions in 1 and 2 below. Match the instructions with the specific information you need to find.

   1 A Which TWO measures to improve staff morale are mentioned in the text?

       B Which TWO measures to improve staff morale are proposed by psychologist Jo Daly?

       C Which TWO of the following statements are true of psychologist Jo Daly?

          i Look for details about Daly's life, experience, plans, achievements, etc.

          ii Look for actions that companies might take to make employees feel happier – although the writer of the text may not agree with these.

          iii Look for actions that companies might take to make employees feel happier – and which Daly definitely supports.

   2 A Which TWO of the following theories about bilingualism in young children have been disproved?

       B Which TWO of the following people have proposed that bilingualism in young children should be discouraged?

       C Which TWO objections does the writer put forward against children being taught in bilingual classrooms?

          i Look for researchers in the passage who don't think it's a good idea for children to be bilingual.

          ii Look for ideas about bilingualism in the text, and phrases used by the writer such as 'researchers now believe this is false'.

          iii Look for statements made by the writer that show his or her opinion about the way children are taught.

2 Now answer questions 23–26.

Questions 23 and 24

*Choose **TWO** letters, **A–E**.*

Write the correct letters in boxes 23 and 24 on your answer sheet.

The list below mentions some things that individuals can do to ensure they get the right amount of sleep.

Which **TWO** of these things are recommended by Matthew Walker?

A   taking a natural product that encourages sleep
B   avoiding looking at brightly lit screens after dark
C   negotiating later start times for work with employers
D   keeping a regular record of hours spent sleeping
E   reducing your activity level at a set time of day

TIP Read the context-setting statement beginning **The list below**. It will tell you which paragraph contains the information you need.

Advice

Each option A–E is based on an idea in the text, but you must choose the options that reflect Matthew Walker's recommendations.

Questions 25 and 26

*Choose **TWO** letters, **A–E**.*

Write the correct letters in boxes 25 and 26 on your answer sheet.

Which **TWO** of the following statements are true of Matthew Walker?

A   He is sometimes reluctant to admit what his profession is.
B   He has based his new book on a series of lectures.
C   He has experienced significant improvements in his health.
D   He has carried out research into the meaning of dreams.
E   He always makes sure he gets enough sleep each night.

TIP The options do not appear in the same order as the information in the text.

TIP Details of Matthew Walker's life, experience, etc. are mentioned throughout the passage. Scan the passage to find his name, and check whether the options provide the same information you see in the text.

Advice

A   Does Matthew Walker always like to talk about his job?
B   What information are we given about his book? And his lectures?
C   Are any details of Walker's own physical health mentioned?
D   What aspect of dreaming is Walker interested in?
E   What are we told about Walker's own sleep routine?

Training Test 2 — Reading Passage 3

> **Review**
> 1. A True / False / Not given task usually tests your understanding of facts.
>   What does a Yes / No / Not given task test?
> 2. Below is a list of tasks you may have to do for 4-option multiple-choice questions.
>   Which of these tasks were in Test 1, Passage 3?
>   - choosing the most appropriate title for the passage
>   - identifying the writer's main point in a particular paragraph
>   - understanding why the writer provided a particular example
>   - recognising the writer's opinion on, or attitude towards, a particular subject
>   - identifying a conclusion that the writer comes to
>   - choosing a summarising statement for the writer's general argument
>   - recognising the writer's intention in a particular paragraph
> 3. What was the other kind of task you did for Test 1, Passage 3?

Task information: *Summary completion (with options)*

When doing a Summary completion task, you need to:
- locate the part of the text that the summary is based on.
- understand the main ideas within that part of the text.
- complete the spaces in a summary by choosing from a set of options.

1 Match phrases 1–8 with the ideas (A–H) which they might refer to in a passage.

1	authorities have reduced the number of parks = **C**	A	Noise pollution
2	the rise in vandalism and petty theft has	B	Recycling facilities
3	job seekers are frustrated by the fact that	C	~~Green areas~~
4	a service not provided by the railway network	D	Employment opportunities
5	thin walls mean sounds from other apartments disturb	E	Population growth
6	these kinds of apartments are too expensive for	F	Affordable housing
7	places where glass, plastic and other materials can be	G	Antisocial behaviour
8	the number of citizens has increased by	H	Public transport

The future of cities

Professor of Urban Planning Sarah Holmes looks at the challenges of urban living

The World Health Organisation has produced a report predicting that 9.8 billion of us will be living on this planet by 2050. Of that number, 72% will be living in urban areas – a higher proportion than ever before. Presented with this information, governments have a duty to consider how best to meet the needs of city residents, and not just for the short-term. Certain problems associated with urban living have been highlighted by research company Richmond-Carver in its latest global survey. At the top of the list of survey respondents' concerns is the fact that competition amongst tenants for rental properties has driven the median price up – so much so people need to hold down two or more jobs to meet all their expenses. Another issue the survey highlighted is the difficulty commuters face. Overcrowding means that seats are often not available on long journeys, but more significant is that schedules are unreliable. Many studies have shown the effect that has on a country's productivity. Interestingly, certain problems seem more common in some cities than others: respondents from increasingly crowded European cities, including Manchester and Barcelona, commented on how their quality of life was affected by loud machinery, other people's music and car alarms. Something the survey failed to ask about was the value people placed on having access to nature in urban neighbourhoods. However, some countries are already moving forward. Singapore is a prime example; its rooftop gardens make the city a far more desirable place to live. It is the Singaporean government that is behind this push for sustainable living.

Perhaps some clearer government direction would benefit other cities. Take New York City, a place where I frequently meet up with other researchers in my field. Luckily for me, I am driven from the airport to the research centre, so do not need to navigate the freeways and constant congestion. Admittedly my experience of the urban lifestyle here is limited to the hotels I stay in, and the blocks within a three-kilometre walk. But whenever I leave my room in search of an outlet providing fruit or anything with nutritional value, none can be found. It seems ridiculous that this should be the case. New York has made great advances in redeveloping its museums and arts centres, but authorities must recognise that people's basic needs must be met first.

Sometimes these basic needs are misunderstood. In some urban areas, new residential developments are provided with security features such as massive metal fences and multiple gates in the belief that these will make residents safer. There is little evidence such steps make a difference in this way, but we do know they make residents feel reluctant to go outside and walk around their neighbourhood. Instead they are more likely to remain inactive indoors. Grassy areas inside fenced developments are hardly used by householders or tenants either. All this adds up to a feeling of being cut off from others.

So where are planners and developers going wrong? Inviting a group of locals to attend a consultation event is the conventional method for discovering what a community might want. The issue here is that it often attracts the same few voices with the same few wishes. But the internet now makes it possible for others to contribute. A community website can be a place where local people propose ideas for making their neighbourhood a better place to live. Developers that pay attention to these ideas can get a clearer picture of the things residents actually want and reduce the risk of throwing away money on things they don't.

An example of a project that truly meets the needs of residents is Container City – a development in London's Docklands area. Constructed from metal containers once used to transport cargo on ships, it is a five-storey architectural masterpiece. The containers have been turned into sunny work studios, and despite their limited size, some come with a bed, shower and kitchen unit. Smart planning and skilful construction mean they take up very little room. Furniture and fittings are made from recycled products. Other countries have their own versions of Container City – Amsterdam and Copenhagen have created container dormitories to house students – but the Docklands site shows how work and living areas can effectively be combined. The units are ideal for young entrepreneurs hoping to establish a business while keeping costs down.

Successful development is taking place in many urban areas around the world, and city planners have a duty to see for themselves the transforming effect this can have on residents' lives. There is no better way to do this than to visit these places in person. These might be neighbourhoods constructed for the first time, or developers might have transformed what was already there. In either case, the idea of cars determining urban planning, and indeed the whole concept of private car ownership, is now outdated and must be abandoned. Instead, the layout of an area under development must make it easier for people to meet up in pedestrianised zones and community spaces. At the heart of the development should be a cultural area, providing venues for art, music and street theatre. Such activities bring communities together, and do far more for positive relations than a new mall or shopping precinct. For this reason, these kinds of performance spaces should be prioritised. Finally, planners and developers must be obliged to create, within the same neighbourhood, different types of homes for wealthy professionals, for families, for the elderly and for young people just starting out. This kind of mix is essential to ensure people can buy a home in an area convenient for work, and for a community to stay alive.

2 Now do the Summary completion task below.

Questions 27–31

*Complete the summary using the list of words, **A–H**, below.*

*Write the correct letter, **A–H**, in boxes 27–31 on your answer sheet.*

Survey on problems facing city dwellers

The World Health Organisation has recently published data concerning **27** .... in cities. This data should indicate to governments that they must think about ways to improve the lives of residents. According to a Richmond-Carver survey, the worst problem facing many city dwellers was **28** .... The survey also indicated that in some cities, poor **29** .... can impact dramatically on the economy. Another issue seems to be **30** ...., although this is more often mentioned by survey participants in European countries. Questions on people's views on the need for **31** .... were unfortunately omitted from the survey, but countries like Singapore already seem to be making progress in this respect.

A noise pollution	B recycling facilities	C green areas
D employment opportunities	E population growth	F affordable housing
G antisocial behaviour	H public transport	

Advice

27 Use **World Health Organisation** as the locating phrase.

28 Make sure you identify **the worst problem** mentioned in the survey.

29 An important word in the summary sentence is **economy**. Find a paraphrase of this in the passage.

30 Check that this is an issue that mainly concerns Europeans in the survey.

31 How has Singapore made progress, according to the writer?

TIP Read the survey title so you know where to look in the passage.

TIP Underline the locating words, e.g. **World Health Organisation**, **Richmond-Carver**.

TIP Look at the language around each space and think how this might be paraphrased in the passage.

TIP Most of the options will fit grammatically into each space – so don't choose an option without checking the passage.

Questions 32-35

*Choose the correct letter, **A**, **B**, **C** or **D**.*

Write the correct letter in boxes 32-35 on your answer sheet.

32 When staying in New York, the writer is frustrated by the fact that
   A healthy food cannot easily be obtained.
   B bad road design causes daily traffic problems.
   C certain venues cannot be reached by foot.
   D visitors are all directed to the same kinds of place.

33 What point does the writer make about the use of security features?
   A It greatly reduces levels of criminal activity.
   B It helps create a sense of community.
   C It discourages people from taking exercise.
   D It creates unnecessary fear among residents.

34 According to the writer, the problem with some planners and developers is that they
   A distrust the use of certain technologies for communication.
   B create buildings using traditional construction methods.
   C tend to put profits before the needs of residents.
   D rely on the opinions of a narrow range of people.

35 What is the writer doing in the fifth paragraph?
   A explaining which construction materials are most sustainable
   B emphasising the importance of clever design in small spaces
   C comparing reasons for choosing to live in an unusual building
   D proposing which specific urban locations should be developed

> **TIP**
> Use the underlined phrases in the questions to help you locate the right part of the passage.

> **Advice**
>
> **32** Make sure you choose an option that the writer expresses frustration about.
>
> **33** Which of these options reflects the writer's personal view?
>
> **34** Although the important words in each option might seem to be **technologies**, **traditional**, **profits** and **opinions**, make sure the whole option reflects the information given in the text.
>
> **35** Underline the verb starting each option. Check that the verb accurately reflects something that the writer does in this paragraph.

Task information: *Yes / No / Not given*

When doing a Yes / No / Not given task, you might be asked to identify:
- the writer's claims, i.e. things that the writer believes to be true (see Test 1, Passage 3).
- the writer's views about a particular idea or subject.

To identify the writer's views, it is important that you can recognise parts of the passage that show opinion, and compare these with the attitudes expressed in the Yes / No / Not given statements.

1 Decide if these pairs of sentences express similar or contradictory views.

1. A The findings now cast doubt on the link between crowded housing and crime rates.
   B Having seen the findings, there is no question that crowded housing and crime rates are connected.

2. A Compared to boys, fewer girls were opting for engineering subjects, a trend that was entirely predictable.
   B It came as a surprise to discover fewer girls were choosing engineering subjects than boys.

3. A Introducing higher taxes on unhealthy food would be a positive step for governments to take.
   B It would be advisable for governments to introduce higher taxes on unhealthy food products.

4. A It now seems highly probable that artificial intelligence will take over the driving in most vehicles.
   B In all likelihood, it appears that most vehicles will be controlled by artificial intelligence.

5. A It is vital that we carry out further research before we can confirm that the treatment is effective.
   B More research should be done so that we are certain that the treatment really works.

2 Now do the *Yes / No / Not given* task below.

Questions 36–40

Do the following statements agree with the views of the writer in Reading Passage 3?

In boxes 36–40 on your answer sheet, write

YES if the statement agrees with the views of the writer

NO if the statement contradicts the views of the writer

NOT GIVEN if it is impossible to say what the writer thinks about this

36 City planners should travel to urban areas that are good models of development.

37 It is easier to plan an entirely new neighbourhood than redevelop an existing one.

38 In future, planners must think about the needs of car drivers as they design urban areas.

39 Cultural venues need to take second place to retail opportunities when developing a neighbourhood.

40 It is important that new housing developments encourage social diversity.

TIP Underline any modals or adjectives showing opinion or attitude.

TIP Don't forget that the statements follow the information in the passage.

Advice

36 The important word here is **travel**.

37 How might **It is easier** be paraphrased in the text?

38 Does the statement express support for the use of cars or argue against it?

39 How might the phrase **take second place** be paraphrased? How might you express the opposite idea?

40 What different kinds of **social diversity** might there be in the passage?

Training Test 2 — Writing Task 1

Review

1. What type of information is Writing Task 1 based on?
2. How many words must you write?
3. Is it helpful to mention your own experience or opinions in Task 1?
4. Can you use an informal style?
5. Is paragraphing important in Task 1?
6. Is range of vocabulary and grammatical structure important?
7. Should you mention specific data, e.g. numbers (or visual content in plans and diagrams)?
8. Do you lose marks if you misinterpret the purpose of the graphic?
9. Should you make comparisons?
10. What should you write about first?

Useful strategies: *Pie charts*

What type of information is represented in a pie chart? How does it differ from that shown in a different type of chart, e.g. a line graph or bar chart?

In IELTS Writing Task 1s based on pie charts, you are usually asked to do two things:

- Describe the simple relative proportions of different sections in both pie charts.
- Compare two or possibly three pie charts showing change through time, or a contrast between, for example, proportions in one institution compared with those in another.

TIP Aim to write more about the *comparisons* than about the proportions in each pie chart.

Look at the Writing Task 1 on page 92. Look carefully at the pie charts and make sure you understand their purpose.

Underline key parts of the task and the chart titles.

Now look at the segments in both charts. Which area of the university's operations received the largest portion of spending in both 2005 and 2015? How would you describe this compared with other areas?

Now compare the two charts and identify how the percentages changed. Mark the segments for 2015, as follows:

- increased ↗
- decreased ↙
- same or similar =

Writing Task 1

You should spend 20 minutes on this task.

The charts below show the proportion of income spent on different areas by one university, in 2005 and 2015.

Summarise the information by selecting and reporting the main features, and make comparisons where relevant.

Write at least 150 words.

Proportion of income spent - 2005
- Financial support for student: 5%
- Libraries: 10%
- Administration and management: 6%
- Maintaining campuses: 10%
- Accommodation: 16%
- Teaching and research: 53%

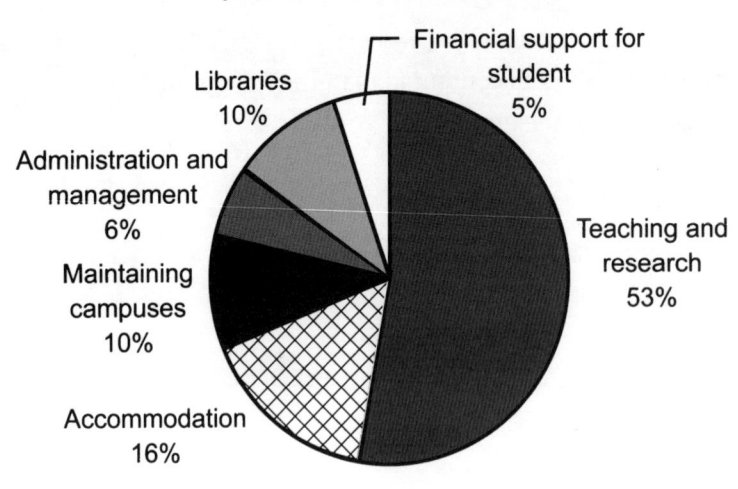

Proportion of income spent - 2015
- Financial support for students: 8%
- Libraries: 5%
- Administration and management: 16%
- Maintaining campuses: 10%
- Accommodation: 8%
- Teaching and research: 48%

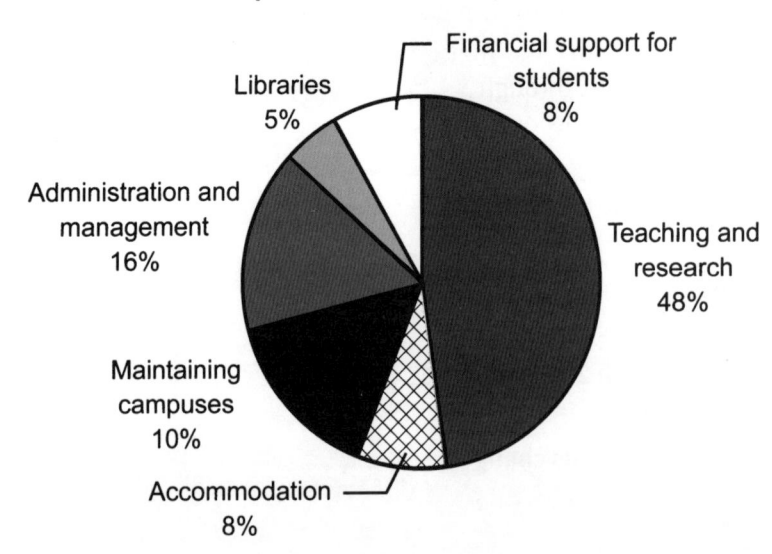

Now look at the sample answer. Identify the following sections:

a Introduction
b Description of simple proportion
c Overview of general pattern
d Striking comparison between 2005 and 2015
e A decrease in percentage
f No change or hardly any change

Sample answer

The charts show how one university spent its income in 2015 compared to 2005, giving the percentages spent on six different areas of its operation. By far the most important outlay by the university in both years was on Teaching and research, and this held steady at approximately half the overall expenditure (53% in 2005 and 48% in 2015). However, there were significant changes across the decade in the proportion of spending in all other areas. The most noteworthy difference was in the portion spent on Administration and management: this increased considerably, from 6% in 2005 to 16% in 2015. Other areas which saw a growth in percentage terms were Maintaining campuses (from 10% to 15%) and Financial support for students, which, though it started from the lowest base (5%) in 2005, outstripped spending on Libraries and accounted for 8% of total expenditure in 2015. Two other areas saw a drop in spending in percentage terms: Libraries and Accommodation, which both saw a halving of their spending, to 5% and 8% respectively.

Which verb form is used throughout the text? Why?

Why does the text refer to the 'proportion of spending' rather than the 'amount of spending'?

Useful language: the introduction

1. Read these six introductions below written by different IELTS candidates. Then answer questions a–c for each introduction. Language errors have been removed so you should focus only on the content of the extracts.

   a Does the writer give an appropriate amount of information about the charts?

   b Does the writer describe rather than interpret the information in the charts accurately?

   c Does the sentence convey to the reader the purpose of the charts?

2. Decide which introduction you think is best. For the other four, think about ways in which they could be improved.

   1 The charts present information about the proportion of income spent in 2005 and 2015 by one university on different areas.

   2 In the charts we can see that Teaching and research was the most important area for spending in both 2005 and 2015.

   3 The charts show how one university spent its income in 2015 compared to 2005, giving the percentages spent on six different areas of its operation.

   4 The charts illustrate how the policies of the university have changed and how it is now spending much more on Administration than on core educational areas such as libraries.

   5 The charts show how much money was spent on six different areas – Teaching, Accommodation, Maintenance, Administration, Libraries and Students – in 2015 compared to 2005.

   6 The charts show spending at one university.

Writing Task 1

Useful strategy: discussing change and similarity

1 Look at the following extracts from answers to *Writing Task 1s* based on pie chart comparisons.

   Decide whether they indicate that a percentage was higher (↗), lower (↙) or remained the same (=).
   1 ... rose sharply ...
   2 ... held steady at approximately 20% ...
   3 ... saw a decline ...
   4 ... remained on exactly the same percentage ...
   5 ... accounted for a considerably lower proportion ...
   6 ... outstripped growth in other areas ...

2 The following sentences were written by good IELTS candidates to describe different charts (not only pie charts).

   Underline the expressions in each one which you think might be useful to use when doing *Writing Task 1s* on different topics.
   1 By far the biggest decline between 1995 and 2015 was in the number of prospective students enquiring about history courses.
   2 The percentage of under-25s in part-time employment increased considerably over the half-century, from 12% in 1960 to 31% in 2010.
   3 The most noteworthy change was in the amount of time given to interview preparation: this rose by a factor of four, from an average of 1.2 hours to 4.8 hours.
   4 Although starting from the lowest base ($20,000) in 1970, average advertising spending targeting 13–19-year-olds had doubled by 1990.
   5 The biggest increase was in spending on rent and mortgage payments, by 10% and 14% respectively.

3 Using the sentences from Exercise 1 as models, expand these notes into full sentences. Add your own places / figures / dates if you wish.
   1 by far / big / decline / applicants / jobs / engineering
   2 percent / elderly / decline / significant / use / public transport
   3 noteworthy / grow / consume / calories / developed countries
   4 high / base / CD sales / half
   5 remarkable / increase / heating / IT / respective

Useful language: 'accounted for' and 'made up'

The phrases 'accounted for' and 'made up' are particularly useful in Writing Task 1 pie chart summaries. Look at the way they're used in the following examples, which are taken from a range of answers on different topics.

1 Buying food accounted for almost 30% of total household spending in both countries.
2 In 2010, children's participation in team games made up a much lower proportion of all sports activity than had been the case in 1980, declining from 38% to just 14%.
3 Financial support for students accounted for just 8% of total expenditure in 2015.

Expand the following notes into full sentences, using the phrase 'accounted for'.
a plastics / 49% / all household waste / 2017
b cars / over / 80% / total number / vehicles / cities
c renewable energy sources / 14.9% / electricity generation / UK / 2013

Exam Practice Test 2 — Writing Task 1

Action plan reminder

1. Look at Writing Task 1 below.
   a. What does the first part of the task tell you?
   b. What three things does the rest of the task remind you to do?
2. Now look at the pie charts.
   a. What do you learn from the titles of the two pie charts?
   b. What do the labels for the sections of the pie charts show?
   c. What do the figures on these labels add up to?
   d. These two charts show a change – is it in time or place?

Before you write

3. Select data which you think is important and make notes on which figures have increased, which have decreased and which have stayed approximately the same.
4. Write your summary.
   a. What should you avoid copying word for word?
   b. Should you try to mention all the data?
   c. Should you say why you think the spending has changed?
   d. Should you evaluate whether the changes are good or bad?

After you write

5. What should you check for when you have finished the essay?

Writing Task 1

You should spend 20 minutes on this task.

The charts below show the proportion of expenditure by students, on average, at one university, in 2000 and 2010.

Summarise the information by selecting and reporting the main features, and make comparisons where relevant.

Write at least 150 words.

Advice

As you read through this unit and other IELTS texts, underline any key words you think you may find difficult to spell in the exam. Record them and practise writing them every few days.

Proportion of expenditure by students - 2000

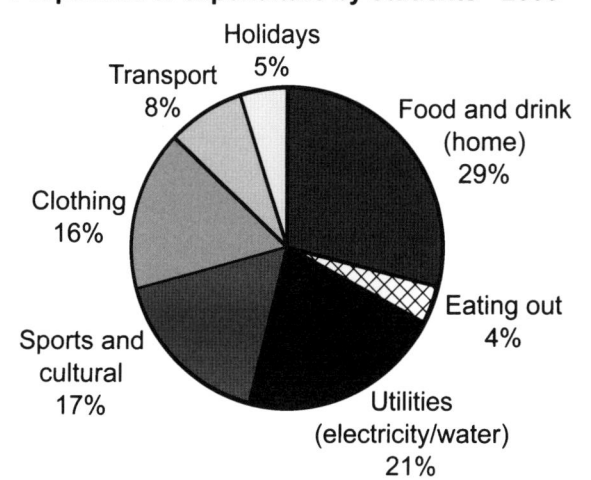

- Holidays 5%
- Transport 8%
- Food and drink (home) 29%
- Eating out 4%
- Utilities (electricity/water) 21%
- Sports and cultural 17%
- Clothing 16%

Proportion of expenditure by students - 2010

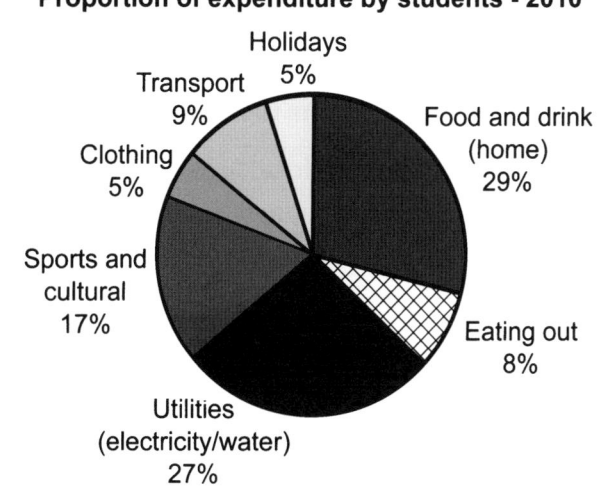

- Holidays 5%
- Transport 9%
- Clothing 5%
- Food and drink (home) 29%
- Eating out 8%
- Utilities (electricity/water) 27%
- Sports and cultural 17%

Training Test 2 — Writing Task 2

Review
1 What kind of writing is in Writing Task 2?
2 How many words should you write?
3 How should you support your opinion?

4 Which of these things does Writing Task 2 test?
- Having correct opinions
- Evaluating ideas
- Stating your own opinion clearly
- General knowledge
- Specialist academic knowledge
- Appropriate style
- Grammar – accuracy and range
- Vocabulary – appropriacy and range
- Spelling, punctuation
- Paragraphing

Useful language: avoiding repetition with reduced noun phrases

To avoid repetition of the word 'people' in 'people who are wealthy' we can say 'the wealthy' or 'the better off'.

For each of the sentences below, replace the words in italics with words or phrases from the box.

| applicants | the better off | consumers | critics | the disabled | the elderly |
| the less well off | the poor | proponents | tax payers | users | the young |

1 It is often easy for *people who are rich* to avoid paying taxes.
2 Many *people who are against this idea* say that it will cause more harm than good.
3 The number of *people who buy things* complaining about unwanted advertising has gone down recently.
4 *People who are relatively poor* tend to suffer more crime than others.
5 Some *people who support* this *proposal* are confident that the measures will reduce street crime.
6 This is likely to affect *people who are under the age of about 20* more than other groups.

Shorten phrases by changing word order and class. For example, *People who use the internet* becomes 'internet users'.

Do the same for these phrases:

7 *people who use the service*
8 *people who drive cars*
9 *people who drive lorries*

Try to reduce phrases by, for example, changing. '*The amount* of fatty food *people consume* must be reduced' to '*Consumption* of fatty food must be reduced.'

Do the same for the phrases in italics in these sentences:

10 *The amount people spend* on IT will go down.
11 *Putting houses up* on farmland must be stopped.

Useful language: hypothetical outcomes: if / when / until

In Writing Task 2 the task sometimes asks you to explore different possible scenarios.

1 Link clauses from each column to form logical sentences.

1	If we do not stop burning fossil fuels	a	more people would avoid paying them.
2	When plastic straws are banned	b	temperatures will rise beyond acceptable limits.
3	A country without strict planning laws	c	always has problems with resource management.
4	If taxes were raised too high	d	there will be a marked improvement in waste management.
5	Until people can be trusted to think of others before themselves	e	local authorities must maintain strict legislation.

Useful language: concession with although / despite

In Writing Task 2 you are frequently asked to discuss both sides of an issue before giving your own opinion. It is therefore helpful to be able to recognise and accept other sides of an argument before giving a different view.

Look at the following sentence.

'*Although* I am a strong supporter of freedom from regulation, I believe planning laws are necessary.'

The word 'Although' could be replaced by 'Despite the fact that', or use 'In spite of being a supporter. . .'.

Join the pairs of clauses below using one of the following:

- although
- despite the fact that
- in spite of + gerund

#	Clause A	Clause B
1	many people will have to pay more tax	most will benefit from improvements in services
2	I believe in rewarding hard work	I feel the wealthy should help the less well off
3	I feel buildings are less important than people	I think there should be limits to construction
4	a widely held view is that crime does not pay	many criminals are never caught

Useful strategy: improving coherence with clear links between different parts of the essay

Read through the following Writing Task 2. Then look at the first part of one candidate's answer in the table below.

Fill in the spaces with suitable words from the box. Underline words which helped identify the correct order.

You should spend 40 minutes on this task.

Write on the following topic:

Some people think that local authorities should control where buildings can be constructed. Others think that everyone should be free to build where they like without obtaining permission.

Discuss both views and give your own opinion.

Give reasons for your answer and include any relevant examples from your own knowledge and experience.

Write at least 250 words.

Essay text		Options
In my own country, there are strict laws about **1**_____ people are allowed to construct new buildings or add to existing ones. There are a number of reasons **2**_____ many people feel such regulations are a good idea. Firstly, proponents believe that planning guarantees that local resources will be controlled properly. It is important, **3**_____, to decide whether there will be enough water to supply the number of new people moving into the area. Secondly, popular areas **4**_____ with a beautiful view might become spoiled if everyone can build there. Related to **5**_____ is the issue of consistency. In a street with a number of historical houses, for instance, it would be damaging to the character **6**_____ to put up brand new houses or to add a new floor to an old house.		**a** such as those **b** where **c** of the area **d** for example **e** why **f** this

The second part of the essay has been jumbled up below. Reorder the sentences to create a coherent argument.

a Local governments are able to understand the bigger picture and take the long view, thinking of the good of the majority in any community both now and into the future.

b Those who take this view say that people are more important than buildings and if, for example, a family needs to extend their home to accommodate more children, there should be the flexibility to allow this.

c However, critics of planning laws feel that the principle of freedom is an important one and that everyone should have the choice to build what they like where they wish.

d On balance, although I am a strong supporter of freedom from regulation in many areas of life, I feel that when it comes to building it is crucial to have strict laws.

Writing Task 2

Training Test 2

Exam Practice Test 2 — Writing Task 2

Action plan reminder

1 Look at Writing Task 2 below and answer these questions.
   a How long should you spend on this task?
   b What are the key words in the task?
   c In this type of IELTS Task 2 you are given two views. Do you have to discuss them both?
   d What must you include in your answer as support for your points?

Before you write
Make notes before you begin to write your essay.
What should your notes include?

After you write

2 Answer these questions.
   1. Should you spend time checking your answer after you finish?
   2. Should you spend time rewriting a neat version of your essay?
   3. Which of the following should you check for?

- Overall structure
- Paragraphing
- Specialist academic ideas
- Signposting
- Idioms and proverbs
- Verb forms
- Formal or neutral style
- Quotations from famous writers
- Linking between ideas
- Subject-verb agreement
- Capital letters at the beginning of sentences and full stops at the end

TIP Make sure your handwriting is clear – it doesn't have to be very neat or elegant but you must be sure that a reader can make sense of it. Don't worry about crossing out and rewriting words, as long as the reader can see what you intend.

TIP Make sure your capital letters look different from lower case letters. It's particularly important that you can show you've used a capital letter at the beginning of sentences.

Writing Task 2

You should spend 40 minutes on this task.

Write on the following topic:

Some people feel that governments should take a large proportion of people's salaries to pay for necessary public services such as roads and schools. Others feel that high taxes are a bad thing.

Discuss both views and give your own opinion.

Give reasons for your answer and include any relevant examples from your own knowledge and experience.

Write at least 250 words.

Training Test 2 — Speaking Parts 1-3

Review Speaking Part 1
1 What kind of topic do you have to talk about in Part 1?
2 What is the first topic?
3 How many different topics will you be asked to talk about?
4 How many questions are there for each topic?
5 What must you take with you to the exam room?

Useful language: where you live

The examiner will either start the test by asking you about your work / studies or about where you live. This could be the city / town you live in or your home – your house / apartment.

1 Think about your home. What can you say about it? Look at the words in the table and add any other words to describe it.

Building	block of apartments apartment on the ground / fifth floor cottage detached / terraced house
Area	a busy / quiet area in the centre of the city in the mountains in a suburb in a village on the coast on a housing estate on the outskirts
Style of home	cosy light modern spacious traditional
Special features	lovely views of … balcony garden gym swimming pool terrace

2 How do you feel about your home? Complete these sentences.
   1 I love my home because it's ....
   2 My home makes me feel ....
   3 My favourite room in my home is ....
   4 The thing I like most about my home is ....
   5 I enjoy spending time at home especially when ....

3 Look at the questions about your home on page 104 and practise answering them. Use some of the words and phrases in Exercises 1 and 2.

Useful language: tenses

The questions in Part 1 are often in the present tense, but other tenses are also used. It is important to listen carefully to the question and use the correct tense in your answer.

1 Complete the questions that go with these answers.
   1 Where ....? I live in the capital city.
   2 How long ....? We've lived in this apartment for 10 years.
   3 Why ....? My father got a new job, so we moved here.
   4 ....? Yes, I'd like to live by the sea one day.
   5 ....? No, I don't think we'll move for a long time.

2 Now answer these questions using the correct tense.
   1 How long have you been studying English? ....
   2 Why did you start learning English? ....
   3 What other language would you like to learn? ....
   4 What do you like most about learning English? ....
   5 Do you think you will live in the UK in the future? ....

TIP Remember to extend your answer by adding a reason or an example.

Useful language: the weather

1 **Think about different weather conditions in your country and how they make you feel.**

sunshine / sunny – happy / hot / tired
rain / rainy – ....
shower / showery – ....
thunderstorm / stormy – ....

clouds / cloudy – ....
fog / foggy – ....
snow / snowy – ....
wind / windy – ....

2 **Look at the questions about the weather on page 104 and the beginnings of the sentences below.**

My favourite kind of weather is when it's . . .
I hate it when it . . .
Cloudy weather really makes me feel . . .

If I'm studying hard I prefer the weather to be . . .
When I was little I loved . . .
I'd really like to live in a country where . . .

3 **Now practise saying your answers. Record yourself and check your answers carefully. Did you use the right tenses? Did you give a reason or example in each answer? Did you speak clearly?**

Review Speaking Part 2

1 Which three things will the examiner give you?
2 How long will you have to prepare?
3 Where should you write any notes?
4 How long should you talk for?
5 When will the examiner ask questions?

Ways to prepare for the talk

In Test 1 we looked at how to make notes in the one-minute preparation time. Making notes is a good strategy but it may not suit everyone. Some people prefer not to write anything. They look at the task and think carefully about each point. Other people like to do other things, such as making a spider diagram.

1 **Here is an exam task. Look at each of the points and think about what you want to say about each one. Don't write anything.**

> *Describe a time when someone gave you some very helpful advice.*
>
> *You should say*
>   *when this happened and where you were*
>   *who the person was*
>   *what advice he or she gave you*
>
> *and explain why the advice you received was very helpful.*

TIP Read the task carefully and pay attention to the key words.

2 **Now look at the empty spider diagram and write a few words in each bubble for each point in the task.**

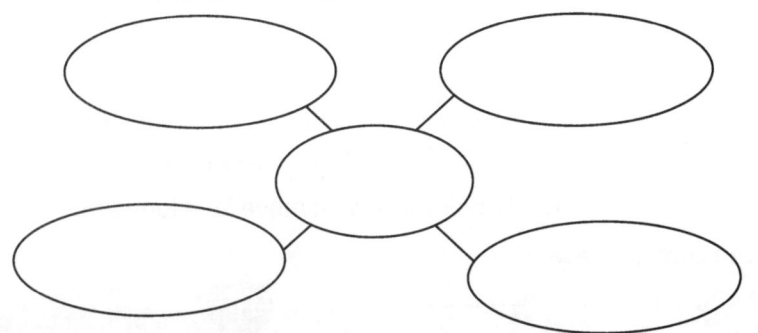

TIP It doesn't matter which order you talk about the different task points but try to give your talk a logical structure.

3 **Give a two-minute talk about the advice you were given.**

4 **Decide which strategy suits you best – making notes, drawing a spider diagram, thinking but not writing anything, or another preparation method.**

Useful strategies: problems and solutions for giving a talk

When you are giving your talk, you may not always be able to find the precise word you want. This happens to everyone and the important thing is not to panic or leave a long silence. There are two things you can do.

Use a 'filler' to give yourself time to think while you search for the word. Here are some examples.

... what I mean to say is ...

... how can I put this ...

... let me think ...

... I'm not quite sure of the word, but ...

If the word still doesn't come, then go around it by using a paraphrase. Here is a paraphrase for the word 'fog': *I really hate the kind of weather, you know when you can't see anything. It can be very dangerous.*

1 **Try making paraphrases for these words.**
   1 an oven ....
   2 a scholarship ....
   3 a guarantee ....
   4 a prize ....
   5 a warning ....

2 **Look at the task about a problem on page 104. Take one minute to prepare using your favourite preparation strategy. Then record yourself giving the talk. Use a timer and make sure you speak for two minutes.**

   TIP If you speak for less than two minutes the examiner will ask you to continue and may suggest you say more about one of the task points.

3 **Look at the two rounding off questions after the task on page 104 and answer them.**

4 **Listen to your talk and answer these questions.**
   - Was there a clear introduction?
   - Were all the four task points covered?
   - Was the vocabulary varied?
   - Were you speaking clearly – too fast or too slowly?
   - Were there any grammar mistakes, e.g. 's' missing at the end of he / she verbs?
   - Was the talk long enough?
   - Were there any spaces where you were searching for words?

5 **Think about the answers to the questions and what you can do to improve your talk. Then record yourself giving the talk again.**

   TIP Don't try to give a talk you have learnt by heart. It will not sound natural and you may talk about something which is not appropriate or relevant. This may affect your marks.

Review Speaking Part 3

1 What topic will the questions be about?
2 Will the questions focus on your personal experience?
3 How many questions will you have to answer?

Useful language: hesitation devices

In Part 2 we looked at phrases that can give you time to think when you're searching for words in the middle of your talk. Other useful phrases can help you while you are trying to think of ideas when the examiner asks you a question, especially if it is one you have never considered before. It is not good to say nothing or just 'um . . . er'.

1 **Look at the hesitation devices in the box. Practise using them when answering the questions below.**

> *Oh, that's an interesting / a difficult question.*
>
> *I've never thought about that, but I'd say . . .*
>
> *Well, on the whole I tend to think that . . .*
>
> *That really depends on the situation, of course, but . . .*
>
> *I think the key thing here is . . .*
>
> *I'm not an expert in . . ., but I suppose that . . .*

1 Do you think young people have fewer problems today than their grandparents did?
2 It's said that the world will run out of food in the next century. What do you think?
3 Will scientists always come up with answers to the problems humanity faces?

Useful language: speaking generally

You are expected to give your opinions on general issues in Part 3 and not to describe personal experiences.

1 **Answer the questions. Start by using a phrase in the box below to introduce a general point and then continue by expressing your own opinion.**

Example: Do people help their neighbours enough nowadays?

'In many cases people are unwilling to help their neighbours because they don't want to interfere. However, I believe that we should always offer to help our neighbours, especially the elderly. After all, they can always say "No, thank you".'

1 Will computer-based learning ever replace classroom teaching?
2 How soon will space tourism become an affordable option?
3 Do international sporting events really help people to understand other cultures or do they increase nationalism?
4 Is there any point in individuals recycling plastic when there's so much plastic waste in the oceans?

In many cases, ...

Generally speaking, ...

Most people accept / recognise / believe that ...

That depends on the circumstances, but ...

It's often said that ...

For some people ...

That can vary according to the culture, but ...

Exam Practice Test 2 — Speaking Parts 1-3

Speaking Part 1

The examiner will start by introducing him / herself and checking your identity. He or she will then ask you some questions about yourself.

Let's talk about where you live. Do you live in a house or an apartment?
How long have you been living in this house / apartment?
What do you like about living in this house / apartment?
Do you think you will move to another place in the future?

TIP: The examiner will record the Speaking test. This is for administrative reasons. Don't pay any attention to the recorder, just look at the examiner.

The examiner will then ask you some questions about one or two other topics, for example:

Let's talk about the weather. What kind of weather did you like best when you were a child?
Does the weather ever affect your mood?
What is the best weather for studying or working?
Would you like to live in a country that has very hot or very cold weather?

TIP: If you can't think of a good example from your own life, imagine a situation that is easy to talk about.

Speaking Part 2

The examiner will give you a topic like the one below and some paper and a pencil.
The examiner will say:

I'm going to give you a topic and I'd like you to talk about it for one to two minutes. Before you talk, you'll have one minute to think about what you're going to say. You can make some notes if you wish. [1 minute]

All right? Remember you have one to two minutes for this, so don't worry if I stop you. I'll tell you when the time is up. Can you start speaking now, please?

> Describe a time when you had a problem and someone helped you.
>
> You should say:
> what the problem was
> who the person was who helped you
> what this person did to help you
>
> and explain how you felt when this person helped you.

TIP: Remember to speak clearly, not too quickly and not too slowly. You will receive a mark for pronunciation and, in particular, how easy it is for the examiner to understand you.

The examiner may ask one or two rounding-off questions when you have finished your talk, for example:

Did you tell your friends about this person who helped you?
Do you often help other people who have problems?

Speaking Part 3

The examiner will ask some general questions connected to the topic in Part 2.
The examiner will say, for example:

We've been talking about a time when you had a problem and someone helped you. I'd like to discuss with you one or two more general questions relating to this. First, let's consider helping in the home.
What can children do to help in the home? How can parents encourage their children to help with daily tasks?
Let's talk about helping in the local community now.
Do you think people help their neighbours enough nowadays?
Finally, let's talk about helping internationally.
Do you agree that everyone should contribute to international charities?

TIP: You can also ask the examiner to repeat or rephrase a question if you're not sure that you've understood all of it. This won't affect your marks.

Exam Practice Test 3 — Listening Part 1

Questions 1–10

Complete the notes below.

Write **ONE WORD AND / OR A NUMBER** for each answer.

Short Film Competition

Rules

- The film must be

  Example answer

  no more than ...20... minutes long.

  submitted before Wednesday, **1** ....

- Don't use any **2** .... with experience.
- For the film, it's necessary to
  include a child or **3** .... this year.

  get permission for any **4** .... used.

  check that English **5** .... contain no mistakes

Advice

- Focus on the **6** .... before doing anything else.
- Stick to a few characters and locations.
- Avoid making a **7** .... because not all the judges will like it.

Last year's competition

- The winner was Greg **8** ....
- The title of Greg's film was **9** ....

Prizes

- Winners receive between $500 and $2000.
- The best films are shown in the **10** .... Theatre.

Exam Practice Test 3 — Listening Part 2

Questions 11–12

Choose TWO letters A–E.

Which **TWO** tasks will volunteers be required to do at Eskdale Wood?

A fix fences
B remove branches
C collect litter
D build bird boxes
E cut down trees

Questions 13–14

Choose TWO letters A–E.

Which **TWO** things must volunteers bring with them?

A gloves
B tools
C snacks
D sunscreen
E boots

Questions 15–20

Complete the flow-chart below.

Choose **SIX** answers from the box and write the correct letter, **A–H**, next to **Questions 15–20**.

A clear photograph
B rough estimate
C new account
D suitable location
E council permit
F basic competition
G good team
H visual guide

To Take Part in the Bird Count

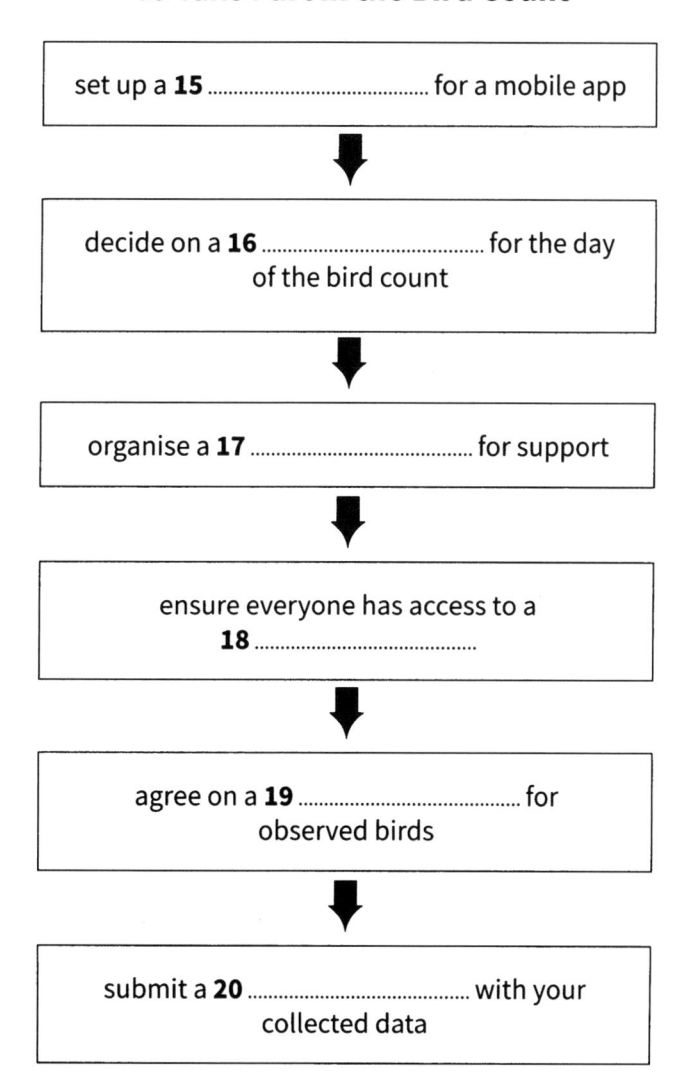

set up a **15** .... for a mobile app

⬇

decide on a **16** .... for the day of the bird count

⬇

organise a **17** .... for support

⬇

ensure everyone has access to a **18** ....

⬇

agree on a **19** .... for observed birds

⬇

submit a **20** .... with your collected data

Listening Part 2

Exam Practice Test 3 — Listening Part 3

Questions 21–25

Choose the correct letter, A, B or C.

Presentation on restoring and reproducing paintings

21 The students agree that the introduction to their presentation should include
   A reasons why paintings need to be restored.
   B examples of poor restoration work.
   C a general description of what restoration involves.

22 When the students visited the museum, they were surprised by
   A the time it took to restore a single painting.
   B the academic backgrounds of the restorers.
   C the materials used in restoration work.

23 What does Oliver say would put him off a career in art restoration?
   A the reaction of the owners of a painting
   B the possibility of working in dangerous conditions
   C the requirement to be able to draw very well

24 What do the students agree about the restored Dutch landscape painting?
   A It shows how taste in art varies amongst different people.
   B It is an example of a work that was once undervalued.
   C It demonstrates how cleaning techniques have greatly improved.

25 What is Oliver's attitude to the digital reproduction of famous paintings?
   A It requires a great deal of skill.
   B There is something dishonest about it.
   C It makes art accessible to more people.

Questions 26–30

What challenge did the Factum Arte team face with reproducing the following paintings?

*Choose **FIVE** answers from the box and write the correct letter, **A–G**, next to **Questions 26–30**.*

Challenges the Factum Arte team faced
A they only had a photo of a badly restored version of the painting
B they needed to see under the damaged surface of the painting
C they had to get permission to analyse a very similar painting
D they had to rely on similar drawings of the same subject
E they had to negotiate with relations of the original artist
F they were unable to view other examples of the artist's work
G they had only limited time to reproduce the painting

Paintings the team wanted to reproduce

26 *Six Sunflowers* ....
27 *The Concert* ....
28 *Portrait of Sir Winston Churchill* ....
29 *The Water Lilies* ....
30 *Myrto* ....

Exam Practice Test 3 — Listening Part 4

Questions 31–40

Complete the notes below.

Write **ONE WORD ONLY** for each answer.

The Challenges of Living in Space

Living on the International Space Station (ISS)

- Astronauts spend months in microgravity, so
  - their blood moves to their head and **31** ....
  - they lose minerals such as **32** ....
  - they have to exercise 2.5 hours to avoid **33** .... loss.
  - they may suffer from poor **34** .... back on Earth.
- NASA continues to improve ways to recycle water, including **35** ....

Building on the moon or Mars

- Engineers and architects must either use materials which
  - are **36** .... enough for transport.
  - can already be found on the moon or Mars.
- Rocks and minerals could be used to make metal, brick and possibly **37** .... for buildings.
- NASA still needs to find a way to make large **38** ....
- People could use virtual reality
  - to visit places like a **39** ....
  - to get a new **40** ....

The History of Modern American Dance

The birth of modern American dance occurred in the first years of the twentieth century. And, perhaps unusually for academics, dance historians hold remarkably similar views when it comes to identifying the individuals and influences that shaped the evolution of modern American dance. Starting in the early 1900s, we can see that dancers quite deliberately moved away from previous approaches. This included rejecting both the formal moves of ballet dancing and the entertainment of vaudeville dancing. As a result, dancers began the new century with a fresh start. One important figure at this time was Loie Fuller, who performed largely with her arms, perhaps because she had limited dance training. Fuller emphasised visual effects rather than storytelling, and pioneered the use of artificial lighting to create shadows while dancing.

Perhaps most influential in the early years was Isadora Duncan, who was well known in both America and Europe. Duncan refused to wear elaborate costumes, preferring to dance in plain dresses and bare feet. She is also notable for preferring music written by classical composers such as Chopin and Beethoven, rather than contemporary compositions. At a similar time, Ruth St Denis was bringing the influence of Eastern cultures to American dance, often performing solo. In 1915, St Denis opened a dance training academy with her husband with the intention of passing on her approach and style to the next generation of American dancers.

By the 1920s, the modern dance movement in America was well established. Audiences were enthusiastic and dancers were increasingly prepared to experiment with new ideas. Martha Graham was one of an important group who emerged in New York. Graham looked within herself to find her dance style, examining how her body moved as she breathed, but also observing the patterns made by her limbs when walking in order to find a new, naturalistic approach to dance. Doris Humphrey wanted her dance to reflect her personal experience of American life. She explored the concept of gravity, allowing her body to fall, only to recover at the last moment. Her book *The Art of Making Dances*, which detailed her approach to dance composition, was highly influential with later generations of dancers.

By the 1930s, modern dance was becoming an accepted, respectable art form. Universities such as Bennington College included modern dance in their performing arts programmes for the first time. In the 1940s, German-born dancer Hanya Holm embraced the changing times by including modern dance in mainstream musicals on the Broadway stage. Among Holm's many other innovations was bringing her own humour to these performances – audiences adored it.

Modern American dance has seldom stood still. Each new generation of dancers either developed the techniques of their teachers or rejected them outright. So by the 1950s the techniques of traditional European ballet dancing were again influential. This was certainly true of Erick Hawkins, who also incorporated Native American and Asian styles. Similarly, Merce Cunningham emphasised the leg actions and flexibility of the spine associated with ballet moves. Paul Taylor preferred his dance to reflect the experiences and interactions of ordinary people going about their everyday lives. Taylor's career was the subject of a documentary that provided valuable insights into this period of dance.

The middle decades of the 20th century were certainly a dynamic time. Increasingly, the modern dance movement recognised and reflected the fact that America was a multi-racial, multi-cultural society. Katherine Dunham, an anthropology graduate, used movements from Pacific, African and Caribbean dance to create her unique style. Pearl Primus was another champion of African dance, which she passed on through her dance school in New York. After retirement she travelled widely to universities throughout America lecturing on ethnic dance, which became her main priority.

Modern dance since the 1980s has become a mix of multiple forms of dance, as well as art more generally. For example, Mark Morris's hugely popular work *The Hard Nut* includes sensational costumes and a stage design inspired by the comics he'd always enjoyed. Another innovator has been Ohad Naharin, who studied in New York and has worked internationally. Naharin's 'Gaga' style is characterised by highly flexible limbs and backbones, while in rehearsal his dancers have no mirrors, feeling their movements from within themselves, a break from traditional dance custom. In many ways it was a fitting end to a 100-year period that had witnessed a transformation in dance. The emergence of modern American dance was very much a 20th-century phenomenon. The style drew on influences from home and abroad and in turn went on to influence global dance culture.

Questions 1-6

Do the following statements agree with the information given in Reading Passage 1?

In boxes 1-6 on your answer sheet, write

TRUE *if the statement agrees with the information*
FALSE *if the statement contradicts the information*
NOT GIVEN *if there is no information on this*

1 Dance historians agree about the development of modern American dance.
2 Dancers in the early 1900s tended to copy the styles of earlier dancers.
3 Loie Fuller preferred to dance alone on stage.
4 Isadora Duncan wore complicated clothing when dancing.
5 Some dancers criticised Isadora Duncan for her choice of music.
6 Ruth St Denis wished to educate others in her style of dancing.

Questions 7-10

Complete the notes below.
Choose **ONE WORD ONLY** *from the passage for each answer.*

Developments in Modern American Dance

1920s-1940s
- Martha Graham based her dance on human actions such as breathing and **7**..............................
- Doris Humphrey wrote an important **8**.............................. about her ideas.
- Dance became a respectable subject to study at university.
- Hanya Holm introduced **9**.............................. into dance and musicals.

1950s-1970s
- Erick Hawkins and Merce Cunningham reintroduced some ballet techniques.
- An influential **10**.............................. outlined the working life of Paul Taylor.

Questions 11-13

Answer the questions below.

Choose **ONE WORD ONLY** *from the passage for each answer.*

11 When Pearl Primus gave up dancing, what did she focus on doing?
12 What was an important influence for Mark Morris's *The Hard Nut*?
13 Dancers working with Ohad Naharin practise without using what?

The Science of Human Laughter

A

Human beings love to laugh. It's such an obvious fact that it's easy to overlook. Laughter, like music and language, is a fundamental human trait. Common sense tells us that laughter is associated with happiness. However, there is also a body of scientific evidence proving that laughter is good for us. Studies show that laughter strengthens relationships in both personal and professional life. It has also been established that laughter improves cardiovascular function, boosts the immune system and releases beneficial hormones into the bloodstream. However, according to psychologist Dr Peter Shrimpton, humans might all laugh, but they often don't remember doing it. 'All the studies show that we laugh more frequently than we realise,' says Dr Shrimpton. 'Perhaps because it is such a basic part of human nature, we tend not to notice when we are laughing.'

B

Infants typically give their first laugh around three to four months of age, long before they can talk. But according to biologists, this isn't because they find something amusing; it is rather a form of non-verbal communication. They laugh to form a closer connection to the people they are with, and adults are little different. 'There is a widespread belief outside the scientific community that we laugh because something is humorous,' says sociologist Jocelyn Barnes. 'While this is true, just as commonly the real purpose of laughter is to promote bonding with other individuals or groups.' This may be partly because it is almost impossible to imitate laughter; even trained actors struggle to mimic a laugh convincingly. So if someone is laughing, the chances are they are being genuine. There's even a difference between a real and a fake smile. In the 19th century, the French neurologist Guillaume Duchenne found that a genuine smile activates the zygomaticus major and orbicularis muscles, and this in turn causes lines to develop called 'crow's feet' at the outside corners of the eyes. No crow's feet appear if the smile is put on.

C

There is certainly nothing new about joking and laughter. Attempts to be humorous have been found from ancient Egypt, dating from 2600 BC. And a long and detailed joke book called *The Laughter Lover*, which was written in ancient Rome, still exists today. While of considerable historical value, it may not be all that amusing any more. A professor of classics, Heinrich Ahrends, has studied many such ancient sources and concluded that tastes in jokes have evolved markedly with the passing of the centuries and that the jokes of our forebears would not get much of a laugh today – and vice versa, no doubt. Nonetheless, studies show that almost everyone can find amusement in some form or other. There is a rare neurological disorder named aphonogelia that prevents some people from laughing out loud. However, they may still be amused or entertained, but just express it in different ways.

D

Much more common is contagious laughter: laughter that spreads uncontrollably between people, sometimes referred to as 'getting the giggles'. Many people will have experienced this themselves, particularly as children, though it also occurs in adults. On one infamous occasion, a group of BBC cricket commentators got the giggles while broadcasting live on radio. And in January 1962 in Tanzania contagious laughter spread through a group of students. Ninety-five pupils were affected and one girl laughed continuously for 16 days. Eventually the situation became so bad that the authorities at the school felt obliged to close it temporarily. In general, however, it is possible for most people to suppress laughter in circumstances where it would be inappropriate. Scientists believe this is possible because in the brain's cerebral cortex there appears to be a laughter switch over which humans have some conscious control.

E

What is becoming clear to scientists is that laughter is highly complex. It appears, for example, that laughter has the power to override other emotions, at least temporarily. Neurologist Nikki Sokolov is studying the network of brain circuits and neurotransmitters that regulate laughter and other emotions. She hopes her work may provide further insights to explain the processes involved when laughter occurs simultaneously with other, seemingly contradictory emotions, such as crying, for example. Another aspect of humour's complexity is that it is so subjective. What makes one person laugh will be met with stony silence by another. Writer David Mackenzie recognised this from the reactions his own jokes received. Intrigued, Mackenzie conducted an international online survey to establish exactly what makes people laugh and what doesn't, and was surprised by the diverse and often contradictory variety of topics and scenarios that were listed in each category. Understanding humour is still as much an art as a science, according to theatre critic Jake Gottlieb. 'Stand-up comedians are a remarkable type,' says Gottlieb. 'Making jokes for a living is a serious business. You need to be a psychologist and social commentator, be empathetic, self-aware, observant, stubborn and have great timing. Not many of us are so multi-talented.' Perhaps not, but we can still enjoy the instinctive humour of our family and friends, and perhaps sometimes buy a ticket for a show.

Questions 14–18

Reading Passage 2 has five paragraphs, **A–E**.

Which paragraph contains the following information?

*Write the correct letter **A–E** in boxes 14–18 on your answer sheet.*

NB You may use any letter more than once.

14   the claim that it is very hard for people to pretend to laugh
15   a reference to research showing that people do not know how often they laugh
16   the reason why people can sometimes stop themselves laughing
17   an outline of the health benefits experienced by people when laughing
18   a reference to a medical condition that stops some people making a noise when laughing

Questions 19–22

Look at the following statements (**Questions 19–22**) and the list of people (**A–E**).

Match each statement with the correct person, **A–E**.

*Write the correct letter, **A–E**, in boxes 19–22 on your answer sheet.*

19   Research has confirmed personal experience by identifying the wide range of subjects and situations that people find funny.
20   Ideas about what is amusing have changed considerably over time.
21   To intentionally make other people laugh requires an unusual combination of skills and characteristics.
22   The reasons why we laugh are sometimes misunderstood by ordinary people.

List of people
A   Dr Peter Shrimpton
B   Jocelyn Barnes
C   Heinrich Ahrends
D   David Mackenzie
E   Jake Gottlieb

Questions 23-26

Complete the sentences below.

Choose **ONE WORD ONLY** from the passage for each answer.

Write your answers in boxes 23-26 on your answer sheet.

23 The French neurologist Guillaume Duchenne showed that if a smile is fake, the skin around a person's .... does not change shape.

24 A .... that was produced in ancient Rome contains early examples of attempts to be funny.

25 In January 1962, an outbreak of mass laughter caused problems in a .... in Tanzania.

26 Neurologist Nikki Sokolov is investigating why .... is possible even when a person finds something funny.

Socially Responsible Businesses

Increasingly, businesses are working to improve their communities, says analyst Pierre Drucker.

Many economies today are witnessing the rise of socially responsible businesses, or SRBs. These are profit-making companies which have the additional goal of improving society in some way. Business commentators usually describe SRBs as a fundamentally 21st-century phenomenon. However, this common generalisation overlooks the significant contribution of Muhammad Yunus, among a number of other entrepreneurs. Yunus established a highly successful bank in Bangladesh in the 1980s lending money to small village business projects that could not attract conventional loans.

There are also those such as CEO Dan Rathbourne who dismiss SRBs as a passing fad which have had little impact on the real world of business. This cynical view is disproved by the evidence: in the UK alone, there are an estimated 80,000 SRBs, turning over about £25 billion a year. What is more, research by the Quorate Group based on interviews with over 5,000 respondents in twelve nations found that not only were consumers prepared to support SRBs but that employees preferred to work for them.

Ten years ago Christine Dubois used her experience in corporate finance to establish the Concern Consultancy, which coordinates advice and funding for SRB start-ups. As professional investors increasingly recognise the potential of SRBs, the number of niche firms such as Dubois's will almost inevitably multiply. Professor of business studies Joel Drew claims that this is partly a consequence of the digital revolution. In his persuasive analysis, digital networks have allowed consumers to identify socially responsible products and services in ways never possible before.

So what are some examples of SRBs? Many that have come to my attention recently are small-scale local companies, such as Renew, which searches demolition sites for old materials – wooden floorboards and other construction timber, for example. Rather than allow these resources to be wasted, the team at Renew have fashioned them into a range of tables, chairs and similar items that are sold at relatively low cost. Other SRBs have rather different goals. The first Indulge café was established by owner Derek Jardine in an area with few local amenities. The idea for the café was to provide a meeting place for local residents – a community hub – not only by serving food and drink but also by running workshops, film evenings and art exhibitions. There are now six Indulge cafés around the country with more planned. Of course, large corporations may not be in a position to change their products or services quickly. But one international telecommunications corporation, for example, enables its employees to take part in the Green Scheme, whereby staff give short periods of their time unpaid to plant trees in conservation areas, and numerous other large companies have similar initiatives.

Another small SRB that caught my eye is Bright Sparks, where engineer Johann Jensen is investigating the use of things such as bamboo and soya beans to make coffee capsules and takeaway cups that will break down and decay naturally. In the longer term, Jensen hopes to work on other kinds of packaging for the food and hospitality industries. Meanwhile, Greater Good is now in its second decade of running a farm-to-table vegetable and fruit delivery box service to inner city residents. Recent years have seen a significant increase in demand for this type of direct service, bypassing traditional retailers.

The increase in the number of such SRBs is associated with the rise of 'conscious consumers', who want to know exactly how the products they buy have been produced. What was the environmental impact? Were workers treated ethically? So the argument is sometimes put forward that SRBs are a response to new consumer values. But equally, many SRBs that I have studied were established by entrepreneurs who wanted to make a difference and have taken consumers along with them. In reality, both sides of the relationship have contributed to the fresh approach.

Consumers, of course, are not always members of the public. Recently I spoke to Lucinda Mitchell, procurement officer for my local council here in London, who told me that her organisation frequently purchases from SRBs because of shared values. Local, state and national authorities have huge purchasing power for both goods and services. And Mitchell's position is becoming commonplace internationally as these bodies are increasingly prepared to work with SRBs, provided they are competitive on price and quality.

In terms of goals, there are numerous types of social benefits that SRBs can hope to achieve. Many concern employment, whether creating opportunities in deprived areas, promoting gender equality in employment or providing jobs for disabled people. Others focus on fair and ethical treatment of employees and trading partners. Some SRBs add additional goals as they develop, which has worked well. Undoubtedly the most common goal, though, is environmental protection. While this is commendable and a reflection of deep concern in contemporary society, it would be good to see greater diversity as the SRB concept evolves.

As with any business, of course, there are issues to be faced. Some SRBs are set up with considerable energy and dedication, but with little knowledge or experience of business, and find it difficult to compete. Some find it a challenge to promote their values successfully and so never gain support from consumers or investors. Others lack an internal organisational structure, which leads to inefficiencies. However, few of these problems relate specifically to SRBs but are witnessed in many start-ups. Greater professionalism and business school education can solve all of these issues, ensuring the sector has a bright future.

Questions 27–31

Do the following statements agree with the claims of the writer in Reading Passage 3?

In boxes 27–31 on your answer sheet, write

- **YES** if the statement agrees with the claims of the writer
- **NO** if the statement contradicts the claims of the writer
- **NOT GIVEN** if it is impossible to say what the writer thinks about this

27 Many business commentators forget the example of Muhammad Yunus.

28 Dan Rathbourne provides an accurate assessment of Socially Responsible Businesses (SRBs).

29 The Quorate Group is a good example of an influential SRB.

30 Few other businesses will wish to follow the example of the Concern Consultancy.

31 Professor Drew has correctly identified one reason for the emergence of SRBs.

Questions 32–36

Complete the summary using the list of words, **A–H**, below.

Write the correct letter, **A–H**, in boxes 32–36 on your answer sheet.

Examples of SRBs

Renew has made a successful business out of designing **32**........................ On the other hand, Indulge wishes to promote **33**........................ and is expanding to new sites. Large corporations cannot always make quick changes but many make provision for **34**........................, such as the Green Scheme.

On a smaller scale, Johann Jensen is experimenting with types of **35**........................ and is planning other ventures. In contrast, an example of a well-established business is Greater Good, which provides **36**........................ to a growing market.

- **A** biodegradable materials
- **B** recycled clothing
- **C** fresh produce
- **D** closer neighbourhoods
- **E** secure accommodation
- **F** affordable furniture
- **G** permanent employment
- **H** volunteer work

Questions 37–40

*Choose the correct answer, **A**, **B**, **C** or **D**.*

Write the correct letter in boxes 37–40 on your answer sheet.

37 When discussing 'conscious consumers' the writer concludes that
   A businesses are slow to respond to consumer demand.
   B consumers and businesses have different interests.
   C businesses and consumers are influencing each other.
   D consumers should put more pressure on businesses.

38 The writer refers to Lucinda Mitchell in order to
   A explain why SRBs lose out to other businesses.
   B exemplify the way governments often support SRBs.
   C contrast the approach of different governments to SRBs.
   D compare the role of SRBs in different regions.

39 What does the writer suggest about the goals of SRBs?
   A SRBs should have a wider range of goals.
   B It is a mistake for an SRB to change goal.
   C Some goals may make an SRB unprofitable.
   D An SRB should not have more than one goal.

40 Which of the following best summarises the writer's argument in the final paragraph?
   A A minority of businesses will inevitably fail.
   B SRBs are more successful than other businesses.
   C Universities should do more research into SRBs.
   D The problems faced by SRBs can be overcome.

Exam Practice Test 3 — Writing Tasks 1–2

Writing Task 1

You should spend 20 minutes on this task.

The chart below shows the percentage of people accessing news via different media in one country in 2013, 2015 and 2017.

Summarise the information by selecting and reporting the main features, and make comparisons where relevant.

Write at least 150 words.

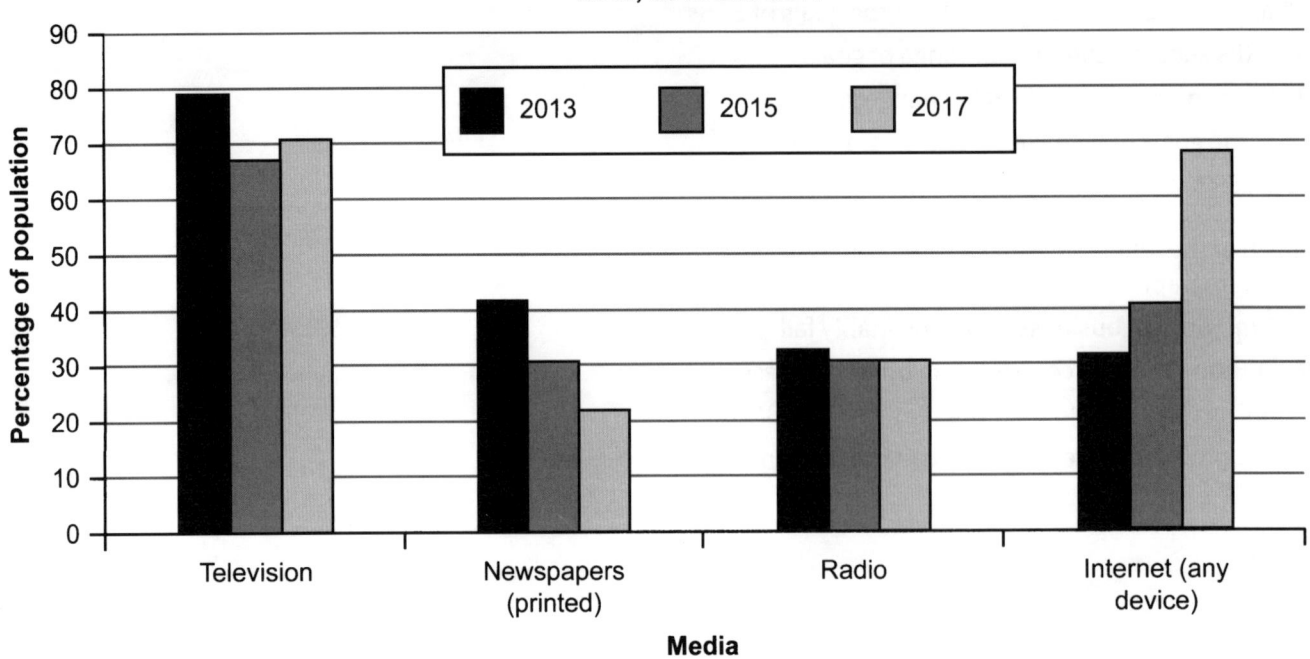

People accessing news via different media, 2013, 2015 and 2017

Writing Task 2

You should spend 40 minutes on this task.

Write on the following topic:

Many people feel it is a waste of money to try to save endangered animal species, for example the tiger or the blue whale.

To what extent do you agree or disagree with this statement?

Give reasons for your answer and include any relevant examples from your own knowledge and experience.

Write at least 250 words.

Exam Practice Test 3 — Speaking Parts 1–3

Speaking Part 1
The examiner will start by introducing him/herself and checking your identity. He or she will then ask you some questions about yourself.

Let's talk about what you do. Do you work or are you a student?

Work
- What job are you doing at the moment?
- What kind of job would you like to do in the future?

Study
- What subjects are you studying at the moment?
- What do you hope to do after you finish your studies?

The examiner will then ask you some questions about one or two other topics, for example:

Let's talk about giving and receiving gifts.
- Do you like choosing gifts for your friends?
- What was the best gift you ever received?

Speaking Part 2
The examiner will give you a topic like the one below and some paper and a pencil.

The examiner will say:

I'm going to give you a topic and I'd like you to talk about it for one to two minutes. Before you talk, you'll have one minute to think about what you're going to say. You can make some notes if you wish. [1 minute]

All right? Remember you have one to two minutes for this, so don't worry if I stop you. I'll tell you when the time is up. Can you start speaking now, please?

> **Describe a place in your country that you would really like to visit**
> You should say:
> where this place is
> how long you would like to spend there
> who you would like to go with
> and explain why you would really like to visit this place in your country.

The examiner may ask one or two rounding-off questions when you have finished your talk, for example:
- Do you think you will visit this place soon?
- Do you enjoy visiting different places?

Speaking Part 3
The examiner will ask some general questions which are connected to the topic in Part 2. You will usually have to answer up to six questions.

The examiner will say, for example:

We've been talking about a place in your country that you would really like to visit. I'd like to discuss with you one or two more general questions relating to this. First, let's consider popular places to visit.
- What are the most popular places to visit in your country?
- Why do many people like to visit historic buildings?
- Why is it hard sometimes to choose a place for a family group to visit?

Let's talk about visiting other countries now.
- What are the main benefits of visiting other countries?
- What preparations do people need to make before they visit another country?

Finally, let's talk about the impact of tourism.
- How can large numbers of tourists affect the environment in some places?
- What could be done to reduce the impact of mass tourism?

Exam Practice Test 4 — Listening Part 1

Questions 1–10

Complete the notes below.

Write **NO MORE THAN TWO WORDS AND / OR A NUMBER** for each answer.

	Island Transport	
Vehicles	**Cost**	**Comments**
Example Motor scooter	**1** $..................... per day	• fun to ride • they provide helmets and **2** .... • don't ride on **3** .... Road
Economy car	$87.80 per day	• four doors, five passengers • can drive on all the roads and to **4** .... for a swim • no **5** .... in the Economy car
E-Bike	**6** $..................... per day	• battery is not very **7** .... • a quality bike with two good **8** .... • a map and **9** .... are provided • no **10** .... is needed

Exam Practice Test 4 — Listening Part 2

Questions 11–15

*Choose the correct letter, **A**, **B** or **C**.*

The Community Garden

11 What was recently discovered at this site?
 A a written text about the area
 B various tools used for farming
 C some drawings showing the garden

12 This location is good for gardening because
 A the weather is warm.
 B there is enough water.
 C it is protected from the wind.

13 In 1860, what was built on this site?
 A a medical centre
 B a type of factory
 C a base for soldiers

14 Today, the fruit and vegetables from the gardens
 A are sold to businesses in the area.
 B are given to certain local people.
 C are used by those who work in the garden.

15 The local college now uses the gardens
 A as a location for scientific research.
 B for educating the wider community.
 C to teach its students gardening skills.

Questions 16–20

Label the map below.

Write the correct letter, **A–H**, next to **Questions 16–20**.

The Community Garden

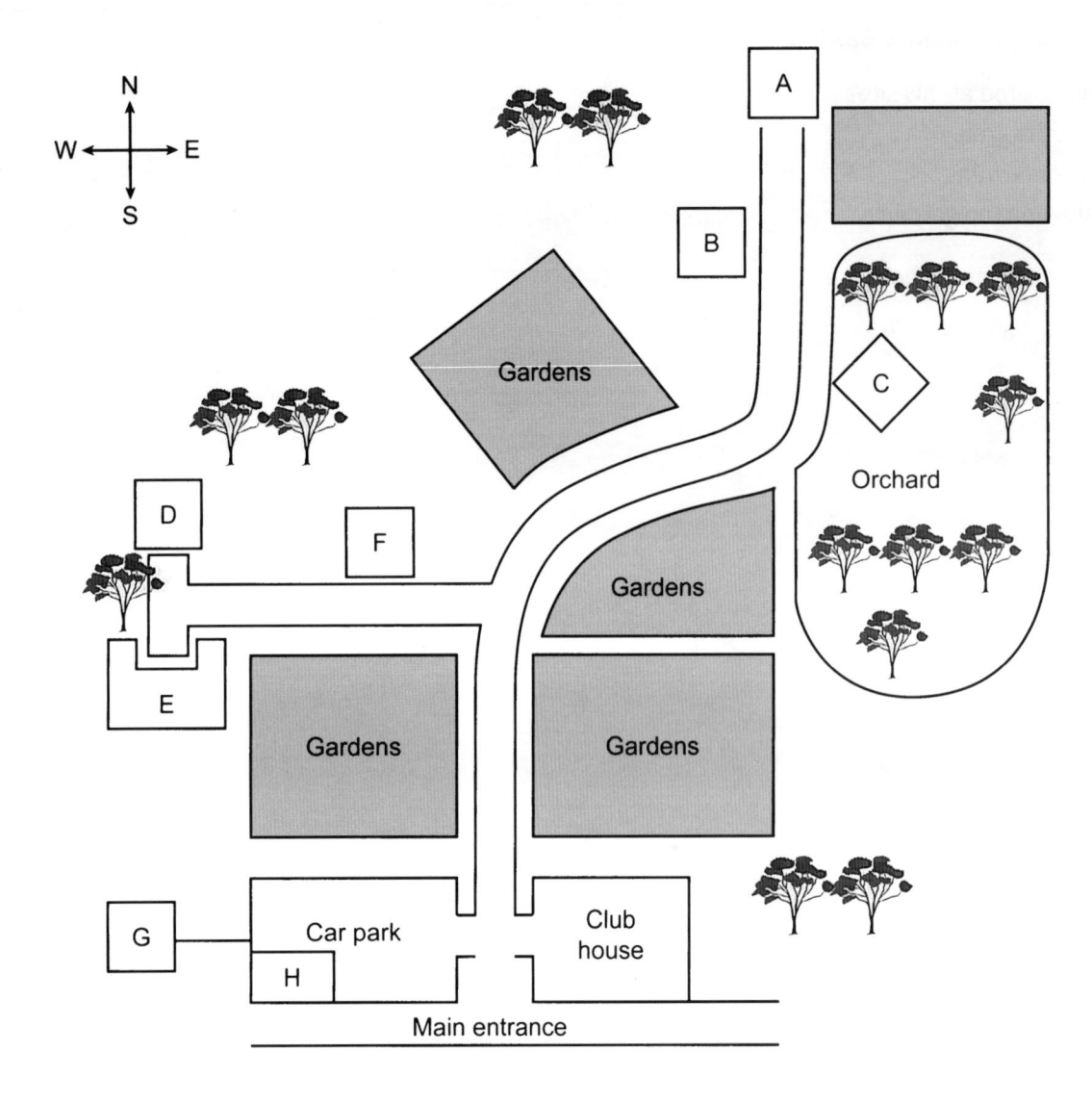

16 worm farms   ....
17 seed store   ....
18 machinery shed   ....
19 compost heaps   ....
20 drying room   ....

Exam Practice Test 4 — Listening Part 3

Questions 21–25

Write the correct letter, A, B or C, next to Questions 21–25.

The Benefits of Playing Video Games

21 According to Alya and Jason, Dr Franklin showed that video games have
   A been used in therapy for a long time.
   B only a limited number of uses in therapy.
   C been accepted by most doctors working in therapy.

22 According to the students, what is the biggest advantage of games in therapy?
   A Some injuries occur less frequently.
   B Costs are lower than other treatments.
   C Patients work harder at their recovery.

23 When discussing the Singapore study, the students disagree about
   A the purpose of the research.
   B the methodology used in the research.
   C the conclusions reached by the researchers.

24 What impresses the students about the anxiety research?
   A the variety of games that were used
   B results were confirmed in another study
   C both patients and their families benefitted

25 The students agree that the Rhode Island research
   A provided reliable evidence.
   B has received widespread publicity.
   C has been criticised by some academics.

Questions 26–30

What opinion do the students express about each research study?

*Choose FIVE answers from the box and write the correct letter, **A–G**, next to **Questions 26–30**.*

Opinions

A the finding may disappoint some businesses
B the finding contradicts other research
C the finding is relevant in particular countries
D the finding is not believable
E the finding is supported by various studies
F the finding is not a surprise
G the finding will become increasingly important

26 surgeon study ....
27 vision study ....
28 sport study ....
29 ageing study ....
30 career study ....

Exam Practice Test 4 — Listening Part 4

Questions 31–40

Complete the notes below.

Write **ONE WORD ONLY** for each answer.

Traditional Polynesian Navigation

Introduction
- the islands of Polynesia are in the Pacific Ocean
- the Polynesian peoples originally migrated from **31** .... to the Pacific islands
- European explorers were impressed that Polynesian canoes were **32** .... than European ships

Equipment on ocean-going canoes
- paddles were used for **33** ....
- sails were made from the pandanus plant
- warm clothes were made from the **34** .... of the paper mulberry tree

How Polynesians navigated at sea
- they did not have the magnetic compass
- they remembered where stars rose and set by making up detailed **35** ....
- when it was cloudy, they found the direction by using **36** ....

Finding new islands
- they could identify certain **37** .... that only live near land
- close to land, they could read changes in the sea's **38** ....

Recent history
- in 1976 the canoe *Hokule'a* sailed from Hawaii to Tahiti without **39** ....
- now replica traditional canoes have sailed across the Pacific and around the world
- as well as sailing, these voyages have created fresh interest in Polynesian culture, music and **40** ....

The Romans Reveal their Secrets

As Katherine Sheen rested on the banks of Hensham river on 3 August 2005, her gaze fell upon a small, dirt-covered object amongst a tangle of tree roots. Cleaning away the soil, she realised it was a leather pouch. It fell apart as Katherine opened it, and the items inside fell to the ground. Although her university degree had merely touched on the Roman occupation of ancient Britain, providing a very general overview of everyday activities, once she'd rubbed off some of the dirt, Katherine immediately identified the coins in her hand as coming from that era. Despite their discoloration, Katherine had no doubt they were historically significant. As soon as she got home, she informed the police of her find.

That might have been the end of the story – except for the fact that the farmer who owned the adjacent field then mentioned the lines of large stones his plough kept running into. By mid-August, with the farmer's permission, a team of archaeologists, led by Professor Kevin Durrand, were camped out in the field. Durrand had previously worked on other projects where pieces of ancient pottery and the discovery of an old sword had led archaeologists to unearth sizeable Roman settlements. He was keen to start excavations at Hensham, and had got funding for a three-month dig. What his team eventually discovered, three weeks into excavations, were the remains of the outer walls of a Roman villa. As many Romans in Britain simply lived in wooden houses with thatched roofs, the family that occupied the villa must have been very wealthy. As the team continued their work, they looked for evidence that might indicate whether the villa had been attacked and purposely demolished, or fallen into such a poor state that it eventually collapsed. Looking at the way a set of slate roof tiles had fallen to the ground, they decided on the latter. What caused the noble Roman family and their servants to abandon the villa remains open to speculation. Another find was six blue beads, crafted from glass, which the archaeologists speculated were part of a necklace. Durrand has previously found gold bracelets on other sites, but for him the beads are no less significant. 'Every find contributes to the story,' he says.

On the outer western wall, the archaeologists uncovered a number of foundation stones. On one is carved what the archaeologists made out to be a Latin inscription. But as the stone itself has endured centuries of erosion, the team has yet to work out what it says. Another find was a section of traditional Roman mosaic. Although incomplete, enough pieces remain to show a geometrical pattern and stylised fish. From this, Durrand assumes that a bath house would have been a feature of the villa. While his team have so far not found any hard proof of this, Durrand is confident it will turn out to be the case.

Something that the team are particularly excited about is evidence of a heating system, which would have served the Roman family and their visitors well in winter months. Although much of the system has long since crumbled at Hensham, Durrand and his team believe it would have been based on a typical Roman hypocaust; they have created a model for visitors to see. The furnace that produced the hot air needed to be kept burning all the time, a task that would have fallen to the villa's slaves. As large branches would have taken too long to produce the heat required, it is more likely that twigs would have been gathered from surrounding woodland instead. Another fuel source used in some Roman hypocausts was charcoal, but evidence for this at Hensham has not presented itself. The underfloor space was made by setting the floor on top of piles of square stones. Known as *pilae*, these stones stood approximately two feet high. The gap this created meant that the hot air coming out of the furnace was not trapped and restricted. Instead its distribution around the *pilae* and under the floor was free flowing. Floor tiles were not placed directly onto the *pilae* but separated by a layer of concrete, or at least a primitive version of it. This would have made the whole structure more solid, and helped reduce the risk of fire spreading to upper levels. The walls of the rooms above the heating system were made of bricks, but the key point here is that they were hollow, in order to allow heat to rise around the rooms and provide insulation. Some have been recovered from the Hensham villa and are now undergoing preservation treatment.

Another feature of the heating system that archaeologists have identified at Hensham was its clay pipes. These were cleverly built into the wall so as not to take up space. The principal reason for including the pipes was to let out air through a vent in the roof once it had cooled down. What the Romans may not have realised, however, was that gas produced by the burning fuel was expelled in this way too. In high doses, it could have been lethal if it had leaked into the upper levels. Inside the rooms in the villa, a layer of plaster would have been applied to the walls and painted in rich colours. Sadly, none of the original plaster at Hensham still exists. However, some of the tiles that the family would have walked on have survived. They would certainly have felt warm underfoot and helped generate an indoor climate that the family could relax in. In its day, the Hensham hypocaust would have been a remarkable piece of engineering.

Questions 1–7

Do the following statements agree with the information given in Reading Passage 1?

In boxes 1–7 on your answer sheet, write

- **TRUE** if the statement agrees with the information
- **FALSE** if the statement contradicts the information
- **NOT GIVEN** if there is no information on this

1. Katherine Sheen's university course looked at Roman life in Britain only briefly.
2. It was clear to Sheen that the contents of the leather pouch were financially valuable.
3. Before excavations started, Kevin Durrand believed they would discover a Roman settlement.
4. Durrand's team eventually concluded that the villa had been deliberately destroyed.
5. The blue beads would once have been owned by a Roman woman of high status.
6. The archaeologists now understand the Roman writing on the foundation stone.
7. In Durrand's opinion, the mosaic strongly suggests that the villa contained a bath house.

Questions 8–13

Label the diagram below.

Choose **NO MORE THAN TWO WORDS** from the passage for each answer.

Write your answers in boxes 8–13 on your answer sheet.

A model of the heating system used at Hensham villa

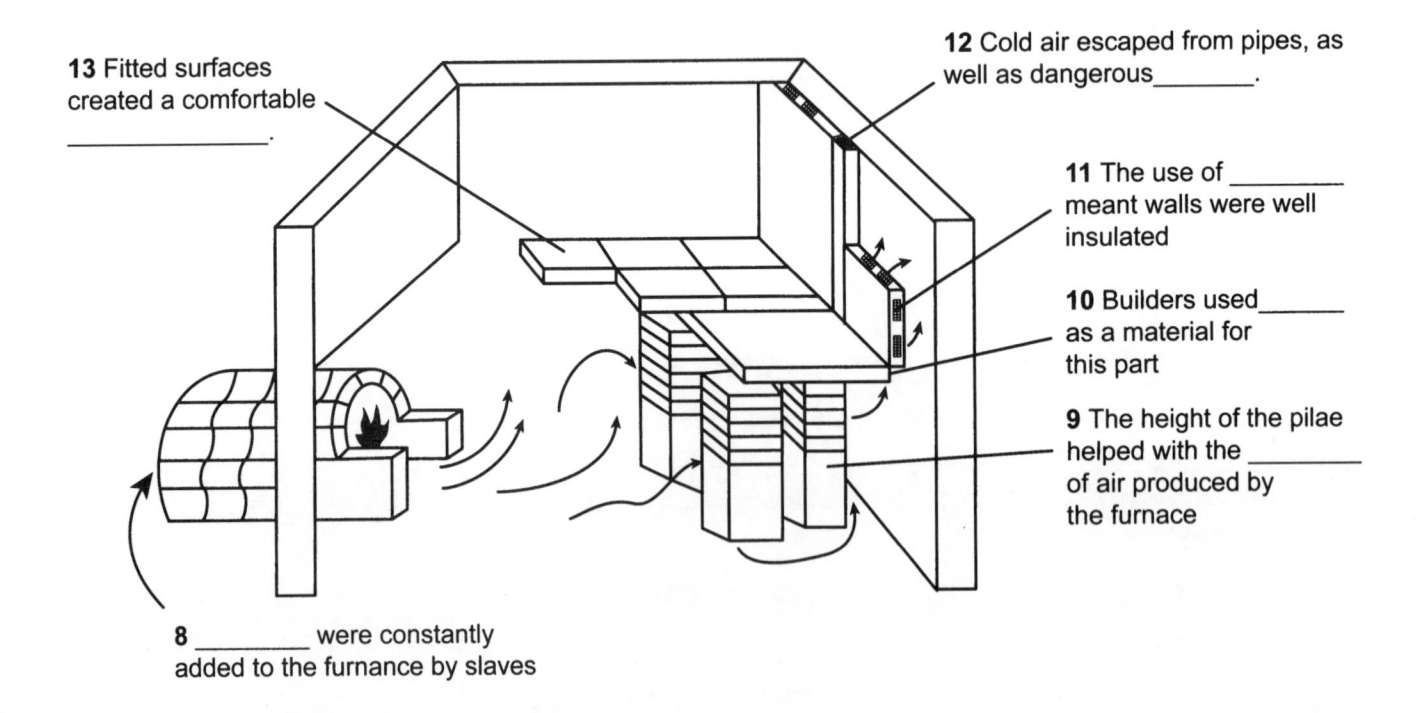

13 Fitted surfaces created a comfortable _____.

12 Cold air escaped from pipes, as well as dangerous _____.

11 The use of _____ meant walls were well insulated

10 Builders used _____ as a material for this part

9 The height of the pilae helped with the _____ of air produced by the furnace

8 _____ were constantly added to the furnace by slaves

Exam Practice Test 4 — Reading Passage 2

*You should spend about 20 minutes on **Questions 14–26**, which are based on Reading Passage 2 below.*

The Truth about Lying

A

An area of scientific study that caught the public imagination during the 1970s involved a gorilla called Koko. Animal psychologist Francine Patterson claimed to have taught Koko a simplified form of American Sign Language, and through signing, Koko could apparently communicate basic ideas such as 'food' and 'more', as well as concepts such as 'good' and 'sorry'. But Koko also used signs to blame other people for damage she had caused herself. While today there is some dispute about whether Koko truly understood the meaning of all the signs she made, Professor Karen Goodger believes she was certainly capable of dishonesty. 'People use words to lie, but for animals with higher brain functions, there's also a higher probability that they'll demonstrate manipulative behaviours. We see this not just in gorillas, but in other creatures with a large neocortex.'

B

Human societies may appear to disapprove of lying, but that doesn't mean we don't all do it. And it seems that the ability, or at least the desire to deceive, starts from an early age. In one study run by psychologist Kang Lee, children were individually brought into a laboratory and asked to face a wall. They were asked to guess what toy one of Lee's fellow researchers had placed on a table behind them – for example, a fluffy cat or dog. The researcher would then announce they had to leave the lab to take a phone call, reminding the child not to turn around. The research team were well aware that many children would be unable to resist peeking at the toy. Secret cameras showed that 30% of two-year-old children lied about not looking. This went up to 50% for three-year-olds and almost 80% of eight-year-olds. Interestingly, whereas the younger children simply named the toy and denied taking a peek, the older ones came up with some interesting reasons to explain how they had identified the toy correctly. Lee is reassured by this trend, seeing it as evidence in each case that the cognitive growth of a human child is progressing as it should. Parents, of course, may not be so pleased.

C

Adults, however, can hardly criticise children. According to Professor Richard Wiseman, it appears that adults typically tell two major lies per day, and that one third of adult conversations contain an element of dishonesty. Other research indicates that spouses lie in one out of every 10 interactions. This probably comes as no surprise to Tali Sharot at University College London, who has run a series of experiments proving we become desensitised to lying over time. She has found that while we might initially experience a sense of shame about small lies, this feeling eventually wears off. The result, Sharot has found, is that we progress to more serious ones.

D

Other researchers, including Tim Levine at the University of Alabama, have analysed our motives for lying. By far the most common is our desire to cover up our own wrongdoing. Second to this are lies we tell to gain economic advantage – we might lie during an interview to increase the chances of getting a job. Interestingly, 'white lies', the kind we tell to avoid hurting people's feelings, account only for a small percentage of our untruths. But if we recognise our own tendency to lie, why don't we recognise it in others? Professor Goodger thinks it has something to do with our strong desire for certain information we hear to be true, even when we might suspect it isn't. This is because we might be 'comforted by others' lies or excited by the promise of a good outcome', Goodger says.

E

We might not expect ordinary people to be good at recognising lies, but what about people whose job it is to investigate the behaviour of others? Paul Ekman is a psychologist from the University of California. As part of his research into deception, he has invited a range of experts to view videos of people telling lies and of others telling the truth. Among the experts have been judges, psychiatrists and people who operate polygraph machines for police investigations. None of these experts have shown they can detect dishonesty any better than people without their experience. Part of the problem is that so many myths still prevail about 'give-away signs' indicating that someone is lying.

F

A common claim, for example, is that liars won't look people in the eye during their explanations or while being questioned. Another is that they are likely to gesture as they tell their story, but so frequently that it seems unnatural – as if they are trying to convince others of their sincerity. However, many researchers have come to reject these ideas, suggesting a more effective approach is to listen to their narration style. A difficulty that liars face is having to remember exactly what they said, which is why they don't provide as many details as a person giving an honest account would. It is also typical of liars to mentally rehearse their story, and this is why one stage follows another in apparently chronological fashion. Honest stories, however, feature revisions and repetition. Recent research has also disproved the widely believed notion that liars have a habit of fidgeting in their seats. Rather, it seems that they keep still, especially in the upper body, possibly hoping to give the impression of self-assurance. Liars also put some psychological distance between themselves and their lies. For that reason, they avoid the use of 'I' when narrating their stories. The reverse is true, however, when people write fake reviews of, say, a hotel or restaurant. In these instances, 'I' features again and again as they attempt to convince us that their experience was real.

Questions 14–18

Reading Passage 2 has six paragraphs, **A–F**.

Which paragraph contains the following information?

*Write the correct letter, **A–F**, in boxes 14–18 on your answer sheet.*

14 details regarding the frequency at which the average person tends to lie

15 a reference to an experiment testing the lie-detecting skills of various professional groups

16 an explanation of why people might frequently refer to themselves when lying

17 examples of the reasons why some people might choose to lie to others

18 a description of an experiment that gave participants the opportunity to lie

Questions 19–22

Look at the following statements (Questions 19–22) and the list of researchers below.

*Match each statement with the correct researcher, **A, B** or **C**.*

*Write the correct letter, **A, B** or **C**, in boxes 19–22 on your answer sheet. You may use any letter more than once.*

19 Guilt often diminishes as people become used to telling lies.

20 People's need to feel reassured and hopeful makes them susceptible to lies.

21 More intelligent species are more likely to be deceptive.

22 The increasing sophistication of lying is part of normal development.

List of researchers
A Karen Goodger
B Kang Lee
C Tali Sharot

Questions 23-26

Complete the summary below.

*Choose **ONE WORD ONLY** from the passage for each answer.*

Write your answers in boxes 23-26 on your answer sheet.

Signs that someone is lying

It is commonly claimed that people who are lying will avoid making eye contact with others and will **23** .... a lot. Many researchers now disagree with these claims. Instead they analyse the way that people tell their stories. For example, liars tend to offer fewer **24** .... than people who are telling the truth. However, each **25** .... of their story seems to be in order, because they have carefully planned what they want to say. And contrary to what many people believe, liars often remain **26** .... as they lie, perhaps in the belief that they will come across as more confident than they really are.

Exam Practice Test 4 — Reading Passage 3

*You should spend about 20 minutes on **Questions 27–40**, which are based on Reading Passage 3 below.*

Review: *The Hidden Life of Trees* by Peter Wohlleben

That so many copies of Peter Wohlleben's book *The Hidden Life of Trees* have been sold is no surprise. Life in the urban jungle can be overwhelming, and many of us long to escape by seeking more natural environments. We hope an encounter with nature might make us feel more 'alive'. Would we use this same term to describe nature itself, though? Forests and the trees that form them are commonly perceived as objects lacking awareness, like rocks or stones. But here, Wohlleben would beg to differ. From his observations, he has concluded that they are conscious in a way we do not fully understand.

In recent decades, a number of writers have investigated our planet's flora. *The Cabaret of Plants* by Richard Mabey and *What a Plant Knows* by Daniel Chamovitz, for example, have done much to reformulate our views about the green world. Central to many of these books is a serious message about sustainability, and *The Hidden Life of Trees* is no exception. What sets it apart is its approach to description: at the start Wohlleben announces that 'When you know that trees . . . have memories and that tree parents live together with their children, then you can no longer just chop them down.' Not everyone will be comfortable with this kind of anthropomorphism.

Nevertheless, Wohlleben's experience of working in a beech forest in the Eifel mountains of Germany may put him in a better position than many to write a book about trees. In the introduction, he explains that he started out as a state-employed forester, taking care of trees purely for industrial reasons. The straighter they were, the more high-quality logs could be sawn. But after a while he began to appreciate trees for more than just their commercial worth. He gives some of the credit for this realisation to the tourists that would come to the forest, who were more enchanted by bent, crooked trees, which did not conform to the straight ideal.

An anecdote that stands out is Wohlleben's encounter with 'the gnarled remains of an enormous tree stump' in the Eifel forest. More than anything else, it was this encounter that prompted him to look further into the hidden behaviour of trees. To his surprise, after scraping at the outside layer of bark covering the stump, he discovered a green layer underneath. This was chlorophyll, the pigment normally produced by living trees. Wohlleben realised that the only way the stump could still be alive was if the surrounding beeches were providing it with a sugar solution through their own roots.

Wohlleben is not the first person to claim that trees are cooperative. In the 1990s, Dr Suzanne Simard realised that fir and birch trees were supplying each other with carbon. Simard's findings made complete sense to Wohlleben, who believes that this kind of nutrient exchange between neighbours is typical of a healthy forest. Wohlleben also had the opportunity to deepen his understanding of tree biology when researchers from Aachen University set up investigative programmes in his beech forest. Discussions with them reinforced his beliefs about the way trees thrived, and Wohlleben eventually found himself strongly opposed to some traditional forestry practices. He finally succeeded in persuading local villagers that the forest should be allowed to return to a natural state: this involved banning the use of machinery for logging, and giving up on pesticides for a start. Since then, Wohlleben has been noting how his beech forest has developed, and his observations formed the foundation for the book. Humour and a straightforward narrative make it instantly appealing to readers without a science background – elements that have successfully been translated into over a dozen languages. Those that *do* have scientific training, however, will be more demanding. Critics of Wohlleben point out that proper academic studies need to be done to prove all his claims are factually accurate. This seems a fair point. What the book will certainly do is transform nature lovers' experiences of a forest walk. Once you know what is happening below ground, you can't help but marvel at the complex life of trees. Will it transform the way we produce timber for the manufacturing industry? As large corporations tend to focus on immediate profits, they are hardly likely to adopt the longer-term practices that Wohlleben recommends.

One of these is allowing trees to grow nearer to each other. This is the opposite of what happens in many state-owned forests, where foresters deliberately space out trees so they can get more sunlight and grow faster. But Wohlleben claims this spacing prevents vital root interaction, and so lowers resistance to drought. Older, established trees, he explains, draw up moisture through their deep roots and provide this to juvenile trees growing below them. Without this assistance, they could die. The relationship between fungi and trees is also given attention. For instance, when pines require more nitrogen, the fungi growing at their base release a poison into the soil. This poison kills many minute organisms, which release nitrogen as they die, and this is absorbed by the trees' roots. In return, the fungi receive photosynthesised sugar from the pines. Then Wohlleben explores the way trees employ scent, giving the example of acacia trees in sub-Saharan Africa. When giraffes begin feeding on an acacia's leaves, the tree emits ethylene gas as a warning to neighbouring acacias. These then pump tannins into their leaves – substances toxic to giraffes. More controversial is Wohlleben's suggestion that trees feel pain. Although scientific research has now established that if branches are broken off or the trunk is hit with an axe, a tree will emit electrical signals from the site of the wound, the application of the concept of 'pain' might be an instance where readers are unconvinced.

Questions 27–30

*Choose the correct letter, **A**, **B**, **C** or **D**.*

Write the correct letter in boxes 27–30 on your answer sheet.

27 What is the reviewer emphasising in the phrase 'Wohlleben would beg to differ'?
  A the fact that trees might not live as passively as we think
  B the idea that a forest trip might increase people's vitality
  C the way that a forest is the key feature of many landscapes
  D the belief that trees exist only for the benefit of humans

28 According to the reviewer, a unique feature of *The Hidden Life of Trees* is
  A its suggestion that ordinary people can act to protect forests.
  B its viewpoint that only certain kinds of tree are worth preserving.
  C its tendency to refer to trees as if they had human qualities.
  D its simplistic rather than academic approach to writing.

29 What are we told about Peter Wohlleben's time as a state-employed forester?
  A He hoped he could make a good living from cutting down trees.
  B He changed his mind about the way in which trees were valuable.
  C He rejected the ideas that visitors to the beech forest put forward.
  D He introduced new techniques for improving the growth of trees.

30 The reviewer mentions the tree stump anecdote in order to
  A question traditional thinking about the way trees grow.
  B explain the motivation behind Wohlleben's area of research.
  C highlight Wohlleben's lack of formal scientific training.
  D suggest how personal stories have brought a dull topic to life.

Questions 31–36

Do the following statements agree with the views of the writer in Reading Passage 3?

In boxes 31–36 on your answer sheet, write

    YES   *if the statement agrees with the views of the writer*
    NO   *if the statement contradicts the views of the writer*
    NOT GIVEN *if it is impossible to say what the writer thinks about this*

31 Wohlleben was sceptical about the results of Dr Suzanne Simard's research.
32 Wohlleben's theories about trees were confirmed after talking to Aachen University scientists.
33 It was a good decision to get rid of machinery and pesticides from the beech forest.
34 The translators of *The Hidden Life of Trees* should be given more recognition for their contribution.
35 Some of Wohlleben's ideas about trees must be investigated further before they can be accepted as true.
36 *The Hidden Life of Trees* is likely to affect how forests are managed by the manufacturing industry.

Questions 37–40

*Complete each sentence with the correct ending, **A–G**, below.*

*Write the correct letter, **A–G**, in boxes 37–40 on your answer sheet.*

37 The distance between trees in state-owned forests
38 The fungi growing at the base of trees
39 The scent sometimes given off by trees
40 The electrical signals sent out by trees

> A may prevent harm occurring to the same tree species.
> B can be the result of different forms of damage.
> C might help the spread of trees in a new location.
> D could be a sign that trees have reached maturity.
> E may affect how vulnerable young trees are during dry periods.
> F can play a part in providing essential nutrients.
> G might encourage disease in trees growing nearby.

Exam Practice Test 4 — Writing Tasks 1-2

Writing Task 1

You should spend 20 minutes on this task.

The graph below shows information about the use of public transport in one country, by age group and location of residence, in 2016.

Summarise the information by selecting and reporting the main features, and make comparisons where relevant.

Write at least 150 words.

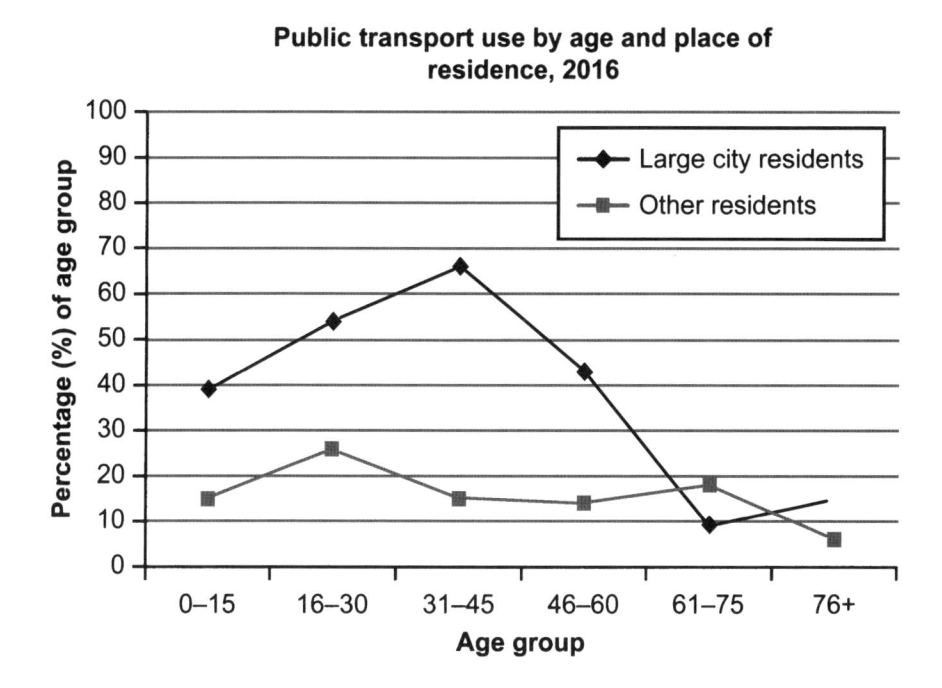

Public transport use by age and place of residence, 2016

A line graph with Percentage (%) of age group on the y-axis (0-100) and Age group on the x-axis (0-15, 16-30, 31-45, 46-60, 61-75, 76+). Two lines: Large city residents and Other residents.

Large city residents: approximately 39, 54, 66, 43, 9, 14.
Other residents: approximately 15, 26, 15, 14, 18, 6.

Writing Task 2

You should spend 40 minutes on this task.

Write on the following topic:

These days it is much easier for many people to travel to different countries for tourism than in the past.

Do the advantages of this development outweigh the disadvantages?

Give reasons for your answer and include any relevant examples from your own knowledge and experience.

Write at least 250 words.

Exam Practice Test 4 — Speaking Parts 1–3

Speaking Part 1

The examiner will start by introducing him / herself and checking your identity. He or she will then ask you some questions about yourself.

Let's talk about where you live.
- Where is your home town/city?
- What's special about your home town/city?
- Would you like to change anything in your home town/city?

The examiner will then ask you some questions about one or two other topics, for example:

Let's talk about parks and gardens.
- How often did you go to a park when you were younger?
- Do you enjoy visiting parks now?
- Do you think your town/city has enough parks and gardens?

Speaking Part 2

The examiner will give you a topic like the one below and some paper and a pencil.

The examiner will say:

I'm going to give you a topic and I'd like you to talk about it for one to two minutes. Before you talk, you'll have one minute to think about what you're going to say. You can make some notes if you wish. [1 minute]

All right? Remember you have one to two minutes for this, so don't worry if I stop you. I'll tell you when the time is up. Can you start speaking now please?

> **Describe the sport that you most like watching**
>
> **You should say:**
> what sport you most like watching
> where you watch this sport
> when you last watched this sport
> and explain why you like watching this sport so much

The examiner may ask one or two rounding-off questions when you have finished your talk, for example:
- Do your family also like watching this sport?
- Do you enjoy playing any sports?

Speaking Part 3

The examiner will ask some general questions which are connected to the topic in Part 2. You will usually have to answer up to six questions.

The examiner will say, for example:

We've been talking about the sport that you most like watching. I'd like to discuss with you one or two more general questions relating to this. First, let's consider playing sports.
- Which sports do many people enjoy playing in your country?
- What can people learn from playing team sports?
- Should all children learn to play sports at school? Why do you think that?

Let's talk about professional sportspeople now.
- Why do you think the top sportspeople are paid so much?
- What are the disadvantages of being a top sportsperson?

Finally, let's talk about extreme sports.
- Why are extreme sports growing in popularity today?
- Many people feel governments should ban the most dangerous extreme sports? Do you agree with that view?

Exam Practice Test 5 — Listening Part 1

Questions 1–10

Complete the form below.

Write **ONE WORD AND / OR A NUMBER** for each answer.

INSURANCE CLAIM FORM

Example
Client details
Name: **Greg** Williams

Policy reference: **1** ....
Address: **2** 102 .... Street, Northbridge
Phone number: **3** ....

Description of damage
Date of incident: Sunday, 17th June
Cause of incident: the house was damaged during a **4** ....
Items client is claiming for:

a pair of child's **5** ....
a new **6** ....
a torn **7** ....
repairs to the door of the **8** ....

Builder dealing with damage
Full name: Steven **9** ....
Client to send in photographs of damaged **10** .... before building work starts

Exam Practice Test 5 — Listening Part 2

Questions 11–12

Which **TWO** opportunities does the Young Explorer Programme offer to participants?

Choose **TWO** letters, **A–E**.

- A Improving negotiation skills
- B Developing supportive relationships
- C Acquiring a new physical skill
- D Learning about environmental issues
- E Competing for an award

Questions 13–14

Which **TWO** subjects must groups study in their preliminary training?

Choose **TWO** letters, **A–E**.

- A Finding sources of water
- B Operating cooking equipment
- C Knowing how to follow a route
- D Searching for safe things to eat
- E Using wood to build shelters

Questions 15–20

What does the speaker say about each of the following tracks?

*Write the correct letter **A**, **B**, **C** or **D** next to **Questions 15–20**.*

Tracks

15 Northface   ....
16 Blue River   ....
17 Pioneer   ....
18 Edgewater   ....
19 Murray   ....
20 Lakeside   ....

A It is likely to be busy.
B It may be unsafe in places.
C It is currently closed to the public.
D It is divided into two sections.

Exam Practice Test 5 — Listening Part 3

Questions 21–26

*Write the correct letter, **A**, **B** or **C**, next to **Questions 21–26**.*

The Future of Work

21 Kiara and Finn agree that the articles they read on the future of work
   A mainly reflect the concerns of older employees.
   B refer to the end of a traditional career path.
   C tend to exaggerate the likely changes.

22 What point does Kiara make about the phrase 'job title'?
   A It is no longer relevant in modern times.
   B It shows colleagues how to interact with each other.
   C It will only apply to people higher up in an organisation.

23 What issue affecting young employees is Finn most concerned about?
   A lack of job security
   B income inequality
   C poor chances of promotion

24 What is Kiara's attitude towards the Richards-Greeves survey on work-life balance?
   A She thinks that the findings are predictable.
   B She is curious about the kind of work the interviewees do.
   C She believes it would be useful to know what the questions were.

25 Finn and Kiara agree that if employees are obliged to learn new skills,
   A they should learn ones which might be useful in another job.
   B they should not be forced to learn them in their own time.
   C they should receive better guidance from training departments.

26 When Finn talks about the impact of mobile technology, Kiara responds by
   A emphasising the possible disadvantages.
   B describing her personal experience.
   C mentioning groups who benefit most from devices.

Questions 27–30

What impact might Artificial Intelligence (AI) have on each of the following professions?

Choose **FOUR** answers from the box and write the correct letter, **A–F**, next to **Questions 27–30**.

Impact of Artificial Intelligence (AI)

A It will give them a greater sense of satisfaction.
B It will encourage them to compete with one another.
C It will reduce the level of stress they have.
D It may eventually lead to their jobs disappearing.
E It could prevent them from coming to harm.
F It will enable them to do tasks they have not trained for.

27 Architects   ....
28 Doctors   ....
29 Lawyers   ....
30 Sports referees   ....

Exam Practice Test 5 — Listening Part 4

Questions 31–40

Complete the notes below.

Write **ONE WORD ONLY** for each answer.

The Klondike Gold Rush of Canada

The gold-seekers' journey to the Klondike river

- Many gold-seekers set off from Skagway in Alaska.
- The White Pass Trail was difficult because of rocks and **31** .... along the way.
- The Chilkoot Trail was very **32** .... so it could take three months.
- On both trails, gold-seekers gave up because of starvation, disease and the fear of **33** ....
- At Lake Bennet, gold-seekers stayed in a **34** .... until spring arrived.
- At Miles Canyon, it was necessary to hire an experienced **35** .... to continue the journey.
- Gold-seekers finally reached Dawson and the Klondike river.

The equipment gold-seekers had to take

- The **36** .... provided gold-seekers with a list.
- The list included
  - clothes, e.g. boots, thick coats
  - tea and food such as **37** ....
  - tools, e.g. rope and several **38** ....

People who became successful because of the gold rush

- Some business-minded people sold supplies or set up hotels.
- Jack London created a sense of **39** .... in his stories.
- Annie Hall Strong and Emma Kelly contributed to various **40** .... in Canada and the US.

Wooden Buildings

Using wood as a construction material for large buildings is an ancient practice. The 67-metre-high Sakyamuni Pagoda in China was constructed in 1056, while Japan's Hōryū-ji Temple is even older, dating from the 7th or 8th century. That these magnificent structures have survived for over a thousand years is evidence of wood's strength and durability as a building material. Still today, 80% of houses in the USA are built of wood. In Australia the proportion is slightly smaller since stone is also a popular choice, particularly in the southern states, while in New Zealand the figure is more like 85%. Certainly, there are problems associated with wooden constructions: wood can rot when exposed to water and is said to be a fire risk. However, with modern technology these issues can be eliminated, which has led to a dramatic renewal of interest in wood as a building material in recent years.

Today, architects and engineers recognise the potential of wood not only for private homes but also for larger multi-storey offices and apartment blocks. In 2015, a 52.8-metre wooden tower block was constructed in Norway, then a world record for an apartment block, but this was soon surpassed by a 53-metre student dormitory at the University of British Columbia in Canada. Then came the 84-metre HoHo building in Vienna, home to a hotel, offices and apartments. Although the HoHo building has a concrete core, most of the structure as well as the floors are built of wood. Many of these advances have been made possible by research at the Technical Institute in Graz, Austria, where new engineering systems based on wood construction have been pioneered.

A good example of these techniques is found at the Wood Innovation and Design Centre at the University of Northern British Columbia, Canada. The first stage in the construction of the building saw large planks of Douglas fir being fastened to one another with glue, which these days can be stronger than nails or screws. This produced large heavy sheets of wooden material; these became the basic structural components for the building. These sheets then had to be precision cut to create the thousands of columns and beams necessary – the team employed lasers for this purpose. Once the cutting work was complete, all the wooden components were taken to the site for assembly. The building was constructed one storey at a time, layer upon layer, not unlike the system used to make a large cake. Once the eighth and final storey was completed, the building reached a height of 30 metres and became a notable landmark in its neighbourhood. And, of course, one of the great advantages of wood comes at the end of a building's life, in around 100 years' time. When the Wood Innovation and Design Centre eventually has to be demolished, it will be possible for its principal building material to be recycled, which is not usually practical with steel or concrete.

Other significant wooden buildings are to be found in locations around the world. Perhaps not surprisingly, given that the Hōryū-ji Temple may be the oldest large wooden building in the world, Japanese engineers are at the forefront of this process. One thing that has been learned from maintaining the Hōryū-ji Temple over many centuries is that it is often simpler to make major repairs to wooden structures than to those made of concrete and steel. Until quite recently, regulations in Japan have made the construction of very large wooden structures difficult. However, in recognition of new technologies, these are being relaxed by the government, with the result that ever more ambitious projects are being announced. Perhaps the most radical example is the proposed Sumitomo Tower, a skyscraper of 70 storeys to be built largely of wood in central Tokyo; its completion date is 2041.

Because wood is more flexible than steel, it has great potential in countries prone to earthquakes, such as Japan and New Zealand. Engineers in New Zealand believe that wood construction can significantly improve building safety in the event of a natural disaster, as has been demonstrated at the new Wynn Williams House. The wood has been left exposed inside the house to showcase how this type of construction provides attractive interiors as well. Another advantage of wood is that it is so light, particularly when compared to steel and concrete. In Australia, the benefits of light weight have been taken advantage of in the city of Melbourne, where a large wooden library has been constructed directly beside water, on land so soft that a heavier building would have been impossible. Furthermore, wood is advantageous even in extreme climates. In Finland, where winter temperatures can fall to -30°C, wood provides all the load-bearing structures for the Puukuokka Block, but also guarantees excellent heat insulation as well.

As wood construction technologies continue to develop, it seems probable that architects and engineers will dream up ever more uses for this practical, flexible and beautiful building material.

Questions 1–4

Do the following statements agree with the information given in Reading Passage 1?

In boxes 1–4 on your answer sheet, write

TRUE　　if the statement agrees with the information
FALSE　　if the statement contradicts the information
NOT GIVEN　　if there is no information on this

1　More houses are built of wood in Australia than in the USA.
2　There are solutions to the problems of building with wood.
3　Several different species of tree were used to construct the HoHo building.
4　Research at the Technical Institute in Graz improved wooden building technology.

Questions 5–8

Complete the flow-chart below.

Write **ONE WORD ONLY** from the passage for each answer.

Write your answers in boxes 5–8 on your answer sheet.

Building the Wood Innovation and Design Centre

| Wooden planks were joined together using **5**.. |

⬇

| **6**.. were then used to cut this material accurately. |

⬇

| The wood was taken to the site. |

⬇

| The building was constructed in the same way a **7**.. is put together. |

⬇

| In about 100 years' time, the wood can be **8**.. |

Questions 9–13

Complete the notes below.

Write **NO MORE THAN TWO WORDS** for each answer.

Write your answers in boxes 9–13 on your answer sheet.

Other Significant Wooden Buildings

Japan
- Experience with the Hōryū-ji Temple proves that **9**.. are easier with wood.
- New technologies and new **10**.. make large buildings such as the Sumitomo Tower possible.

Other countries
- Wynn Williams House in New Zealand is earthquake-proof and is an example of how wooden buildings can have **11**..
- Wood is so light that a new library in Australia was built right next to **12**..
- Finland's Puukuokka Block illustrates that wood provides good **13**.. in addition to structural strength.

Exam Practice Test 5 — Reading Passage 2

*You should spend about 20 minutes on **Questions 14–26**, which are based on Reading Passage 2 below.*

Questions 14–19

Reading Passage 2 has six paragraphs, **A–F**.

Choose the correct heading for each paragraph from the list of headings below.

*Write the correct number, **i–viii**, in boxes 14–19 on your answer sheet.*

List of Headings

- i AI can improve the profitability of sporting businesses
- ii Responses to criticisms of AI in sports coaching
- iii A contrast between coaching today and in the past
- iv An academic outlines some of the advantages of AI in sport
- v The businesses responsible for creating AI software
- vi The use of AI to decide the results of a competition
- vii An academic study into a team sport in one country
- viii The uses of AI in coaching a range of different sports

14 Paragraph A ....
15 Paragraph B ....
16 Paragraph C ....
17 Paragraph D ....
18 Paragraph E ....
19 Paragraph F ....

Artificial Intelligence in Sport

A

The first sports game was televised in the USA more than fifty years ago. Over the following decades television provided sports coaches with a wealth of information to analyse. By viewing recordings, they could study the number of passes received, tackles avoided, distances covered, speeds achieved and a host of other factors relating to the performance of their teams or athletes. Most of this data, though, consisted of bare statistics without any meaningful context. However, the use of artificial intelligence (AI) is now enabling an alternative approach to coaching. AI means the development of computer systems that can perform tasks usually associated with human intelligence, such as decision making. Increasingly, computers are being trained to understand the rules and objectives of sports so they can coach more directly. AI can analyse not only a player's actions, but also relate those actions to the wider context, including the directives of the coach and the actions of other players. Sports scientists believe that AI is revolutionising sports coaching by analysing patterns of behaviour in ways simply not possible before.

B

There may be limitless ways in which AI technology can be developed, but certain practical applications are already apparent. Recently, a research experiment was conducted into the Spanish football league using an AI algorithm to analyse the passing strategies of 20 teams. The research revealed that two teams, Barcelona and Real Madrid, had more than 150 recurring passing patterns. However, the algorithm detected just 31 passing patterns used by Atlético Madrid. All of Atlético's other plays were one-offs that were never repeated, and the team won the league that season. One conclusion seems to be that teams with a less predictable style of play win more games. What's more, according to Dr Johann Muller, a sports scientist who has studied the Spanish research findings, the number of injuries a team suffers increases when they play in a style that prioritises offence.

C

Since then, there has been a great deal of interest in the potential of AI. Professor of sports education Rebecca Graves believes that AI can provide coaches with invaluable insights. 'Tactics were once closely guarded secrets,' says Professor Graves, 'but now a coach with access to AI can identify how a rival team is likely to play a match based on historic form. Once this was largely guesswork but now it can be achieved with some confidence.' The expense of AI technology means it will probably remain beyond the reach of all but elite teams, but among this group the implications are enormous. Professor Graves argues that AI allows preparations for a match to be tailored to individual players with much greater precision. She identifies fitness work, skills development, diet and numerous other factors that can be minutely customised, based on an individual's particular strengths and weaknesses.

D

Part of the appeal of AI lies in its versatility. Ice hockey coaches in Finland are using AI to analyse the success of different plays. An Indian company has employed wearable technology developed in other fields to analyse stride patterns. This analysis has allowed its technicians to develop sneakers in various styles aimed at both long- and short-distance runners. Coaching practices in professional basketball, American football and tennis are also being transformed by AI. In addition, the technology has applications in highly technical sports such as car racing. Coaches involved in the National Association for Stock Car Auto Racing (NASCAR) believe that AI algorithms not only help drivers go faster but also enhance the safety of the sport because of their ability to monitor and predict potential problems.

E

AI doesn't get tired, has extraordinary powers of vision, particularly for objects moving at speed, and is capable of making complex calculations very quickly. For all these reasons AI is increasingly being used in the high-pressure world of judging gymnastics performances.

Research has shown that, particularly over a whole day's worth of events, computers are just as reliable as human judges when it comes to giving gymnasts a score. However, computer scientist Henri Simeonson has been quick to warn about some potential difficulties. In particular, Simeonson is concerned that AI is vulnerable to hackers, who might be able to influence the outcome of a tournament.

F

It should not be forgotten, either, that many sports stars and sports teams are commercially dependent on their fans. If sufficient supporters do not buy tickets to games or pay to view a recording, the teams might struggle to survive. But now teams and stars are making increasing use of chatbots and other 'virtual assistants' to provide fans with statistics, news and background information about their favourite players. Another innovation is seen in Minor League Baseball in the USA, which is promoting the sport and seeking new fans with the use of AI-enhanced journalism. In this way baseball is keeping supporters informed with all the up-to-the-minute developments in ways not possible with more traditional approaches. Analysts believe these sorts of initiatives are crucial to increasing a player or team's revenue stream. It's just one more way that sports stand to benefit from AI technologies, on and off the field.

Questions 20 and 21

The list below gives some ways coaches could use AI.

*Choose **TWO** letters, **A-E**.*

Write the correct letters in boxes 20 and 21 on your answer sheet.

Which **TWO** of these are proposed by Professor Rebecca Graves?

- **A** speeding up analysis of data
- **B** personalising training programmes
- **C** improving mental toughness
- **D** reducing cost of sports coaching
- **E** identifying opponents' game plans

Questions 22-26

Complete the sentences below.

*Choose **ONE WORD ONLY** from the passage for each answer.*

Write your answers in boxes 22-26 on your answer sheet.

22 Analysis of AI data by Dr Johann Muller suggests that teams which play defensively have fewer ....

23 An Indian company has designed new .... using AI technology.

24 The use of AI in NASCAR is believed to improve .... as well as driver performance.

25 Henri Simeonson says that .... might be able to disrupt AI and make competitions unfair.

26 In Minor League Baseball, a type of .... powered by AI is giving the sport greater publicity.

The Influence of the Crime Writer Agatha Christie

Crime fiction books, in which detectives hunt for the perpetrators of crimes, have been popular with readers for many decades – so popular, in fact, that at a recent London Book Fair sales of the genre overtook general fiction for the first time ever, a development that had been widely anticipated. Commercial success, of course, does not impress everyone and there are those who believe crime fiction should not be held in such high regard. Prominent in this group is Sebastian Franklin, who has argued that most crime fiction books better resemble crossword puzzles than literature. His view is shared by other literary critics. However, increasingly this is a minority opinion as crime fiction becomes recognised around the world as a rich and dynamic literary genre in its own right.

Crime writing really came to prominence in the 1920s and 30s with the books of the British author Agatha Christie, and to a slightly lesser extent the American James M. Cain. Agatha Christie was a prolific writer, publishing more than 60 detective novels over a 50-year period, beginning in 1920. However, the majority of the general public have never picked up one of her books and are more familiar with Christie from the numerous adaptations of her work for films. The colourful locations around the world where Christie set many of her stories were not fictional depictions, but were informed by her extensive travels, on the Orient Express train, to Cairo and the River Nile, and elsewhere. Her memoir, *Come, Tell Me How You Live*, published in 1946, is a non-fiction account of these real-life travels, so is unique among Christie's publications. Success brought Christie considerable wealth and international fame, though she never lost her appetite for work, continuing writing and publishing until shortly before her death in 1976.

Without doubt there are certain elements that tend to be repeated in Christie's books. The stories generally revolve around a well-off if not aristocratic circle of people, whose privileged lives are thrown into chaos by an unexplained crime. What's more, the location is often a confined space of some sort: a train, an island, a boat, an isolated house or a village. This is quite different, for example, to the world of the fictional detective Sherlock Holmes, who often has as his hunting ground the entire city of London. But the influence of Christie's sheltered, secluded locations has been immense, for they have been used in countless television series ever since.

The writer Michael Utley argues that Christie's characters lack depth and are not convincing people we can believe in. This is a not infrequent complaint, but it is quite untrue. Christie was a perceptive observer of human nature and psychology and she put the traits of people she knew into many of her fictional characters. Part of the reason her appeal has been so widespread is that she wrote about human relationships in a way so many of us can relate to. Her very first book, *The Mysterious Affair at Styles*, features the amateur detective Hercule Poirot. Poirot and Miss Marple are Christie's two best known and most frequently imitated characters precisely because they are so well drawn and believable. Further evidence of Christie's ability at characterisation was provided by a recent survey. The survey asked readers to identify the villain revealed in the final pages of Christie's sixteenth book, *Murder on the Orient Express*. Most readers could not recall, because for them the really important aspect of the book had been the interplay between the characters, not the outcome. The truth is that Christie's characters were one of her greatest achievements as a writer.

The books are also action-packed, no less so than today's most popular thrillers. Christie mastered the art of the page-turner: events unfold so quickly and unpredictably that we keep reading to find out what happens next. The most significant consequence is that it is so simple to overlook vital clues. It is worth reading a Christie book a second time just to notice how carefully she hides crucial information about the criminal's identity. It was there all along, but we just fail to see it because she has created such tension and so many exciting distractions.

Attempts to retell Christie's stories in contemporary times have largely been unsuccessful; they work best in their original early twentieth-century settings and cannot accommodate mobile phones, computers and DNA analysis. But that does not mean her influence has come to an end. Indeed, a new generation of global crime writers is emerging in nations as diverse as Brazil, Singapore, South Korea, India and Nigeria, to name but five. And though each new writer adds something of their own, they all employ conventions first established by Christie. If we take just one of her books, *The Murder of Roger Ackroyd*, we find near perfect examples of conventions that are still used today: tight plotting, clever sub-plots, unexpected twists, perceptive characterisation. Perhaps this is why Christie herself is believed to have ranked *The Murder of Roger Ackroyd* above all her other work. Certainly, the digital revolution has transformed crime fighting. But a survey of contemporary crime writing shows that Agatha Christie's legacy is more important now than at any time previously, at the very point when crime writing has become the most popular of all book genres.

Questions 27–32

Do the following statements agree with the claims of the writer in Reading Passage 3?

In boxes 27–32 on your answer sheet, write

    YES   *if the statement agrees with the claims of the writer*
    NO   *if the statement contradicts the claims of the writer*
    NOT GIVEN *if it is impossible to say what the writer thinks about this*

27 Sales of crime fiction were surprisingly high at a recent London Book Fair.
28 Literary critics such as Sebastian Franklin think that crime fiction is overrated.
29 Agatha Christie and James M. Cain admired each other's writing.
30 Most people know about Christie from films rather than books.
31 Christie's descriptions of international locations were based on her own experience.
32 Christie enjoyed the wealth and fame she achieved through writing.

Questions 33–36

*Choose the correct answer, **A**, **B**, **C** or **D**.*

Write the correct letter in boxes 33–36 on your answer sheet.

33 What is the writer doing in the third paragraph?
    A discussing one weakness of Christie's style
    B identifying a writer who influenced Christie
    C contrasting different techniques Christie used
    D listing some features of a typical Christie story

34 The writer refers to Michael Utley in order to
    A reject a common criticism of Christie's books.
    B compare two of Christie's better-known books.
    C explain the conclusion of one of Christie's books.
    D suggest that each of Christie's books was different.

35 What point does the writer make about Christie's writing style in the fifth paragraph?
    A Occasionally, the stories do not make sense.
    B Little happens compared to modern stories.
    C Important evidence is very easy to miss.
    D Some unnecessary details are included.

36 What does the writer conclude about Christie in the final paragraph?
    A Her influence is slowly beginning to decrease.
    B She is more influential today than ever before.
    C One book was more influential than the others.
    D She has only influenced writers in certain countries.

Questions 37–40

*Complete each sentence with the correct ending, **A–F**, below.*

*Write the correct letter, **A–F**, in boxes 37–40 on your answer sheet.*

37 Christie's book *Come, Tell Me How You Live*,
38 Christie's first book, *The Mysterious Affair at Styles*
39 Christie's sixteenth book, *Murder on the Orient Express*
40 *The Murder of Roger Ackroyd*, published in 1926,

A is an example of a book disliked by many critics.
B has sold more copies than her other books.
C has illustrated the fact that readers cannot remember the ending.
D was Christie's own favourite from among her books for good reasons.
E is different from all of her other books.
F introduced one of her most famous and most often copied characters.

Exam Practice Test 5 — Writing Tasks 1-2

Writing Task 1

You should spend 20 minutes on this task.

The table below shows how patients evaluated different services at three health centres.

Summarise the information by selecting and reporting the main features, and make comparisons where relevant.

Write at least 150 words.

How patients evaluated health centre services

Aspect of service	(1 = very poor; 10 = excellent)		
	Longston Centre	Peveril Centre	Marchbank Centre
Booking appointments	5.2	9.1	7.8
Doctors' service	8.0	8.7	8.4
Care of children	6.3	7.5	7.3
Pharmacy	5.1	6.3	5.8
Response to concerns	4.3	9.6	6.5
Overall average	**5.8**	**8.3**	**7.2**

Writing Task 2

You should spend 40 minutes on this task.

Write on the following topic:

Scientific developments in farming always bring major benefits.

To what extent do you agree or disagree with this statement?

Give reasons for your answer and include any relevant examples from your own knowledge and experience.

Write at least 250 words.

Exam Practice Test 5 — Speaking Parts 1–3

Speaking Part 1

The examiner will start by introducing him/herself and checking your identity. He or she will then ask you some questions about yourself and then go on to ask you some questions about one or two other topics, for example:

Let's talk about mobile/cell phones.

- When did you get your first mobile/cell phone?
- How often do you change your mobile/cell phone?
- What do you use it for most often?
- Do you think you could live without a mobile/cell phone?

or

Let's talk about concentrating.

- When do you need to concentrate most?
- Do you ever find it difficult to concentrate?
- What do you do to help you concentrate?
- Did you find it easier or harder to concentrate when you were younger?

Speaking Part 2

The examiner will give you a topic like the one below and some paper and a pencil.

The examiner will say:

I'm going to give you a topic and I'd like you to talk about it for one to two minutes. Before you talk, you'll have one minute to think about what you're going to say. You can make some notes if you wish. [1 minute]

All right? Remember you have one to two minutes for this, so don't worry if I stop you. I'll tell you when the time is up. Can you start speaking now, please?

> **Describe a person you know who has an interesting job.**
>
> **You should say:**
> **who the person is**
> **what job the person does**
> **what skills he or she needs to do this job**
>
> **and explain why you think this person's job is interesting.**

The examiner may ask one or two rounding-off questions when you have finished your talk, for example:
- Have you told other people about this person?
- Do you think you would be good at this person's job?

Speaking Part 3

The examiner will ask some general questions which are connected to the topic in Part 2. You will usually have to answer up to six questions.

The examiner will say, for example:

We've been talking about a person you know who has an interesting job. I'd like to discuss with you one or two more general questions relating to this. First, let's consider choosing a job.

- Who can best advise young people about jobs, parents or teachers? Why?
- What is the most important thing to consider when choosing a job?

Let's talk about different ways of working now.

- Is it better to work for a small company or a large international company? Why?
- What are the advantages and disadvantages of working from home?

Finally, let's talk about having a successful career.

- Many people say that learning from mistakes is the key to a successful career. Do you agree with this view?
- How easy is it for people who want a successful career to balance their work and personal life?

Exam Practice Test 6 — Listening Part 1

Questions 1–10

Complete the table below.

Write **ONE WORD ONLY AND / OR A NUMBER** for each answer.

Kingstown Tours

Name of tour	Price	Main activities	Other information
Cave Explorers	*Example* $93	• go in a small **1** .... to the other side of the lake • explore the caves	• minimum age of **2** .... years
Silver Fjord	$220	• travel by **3** .... to the fjord • at Easten go for a **4** .... • cruise on the fjord • see mountains and a large **5**	• eat a barbecue lunch • see marine life such as seals and **6** ....
High Country	$105	• visit a historic home • lunch is in the **7** .... • in the afternoon visit a **8**	• this tour has excellent reviews
Zipline	$75	• travel on a zipline above an old **9**	• reach speeds of **10** .... miles per hour

Exam Practice Test 6 — Listening Part 2

Questions 11–15

Choose the correct letter, A, B or C.

Willford Living Museum

11 In the early 1800s most land in Willford was
   A occupied by houses.
   B used for farming.
   C covered in trees.

12 What happened in 1830 in Willford?
   A Ships started to be built nearby.
   B The first trains arrived in the town.
   C Valuable substances were found underground.

13 By the 1870s Willford was most famous for making
   A various metal objects.
   B all types of clothing.
   C plates and cups.

14 What does the guide say about visitors to the museum these days?
   A 900 visitors enter on a typical day.
   B 7,600 visitors arrive every week.
   C 300,000 visitors come each year.

15 The museum is also sometimes used
   A as a location for filming.
   B for business conferences.
   C by people getting married.

Questions 16–20

Label the map below.

Write the correct letter, **A–H**, next to **Questions 16–20**.

Willford Living Museum

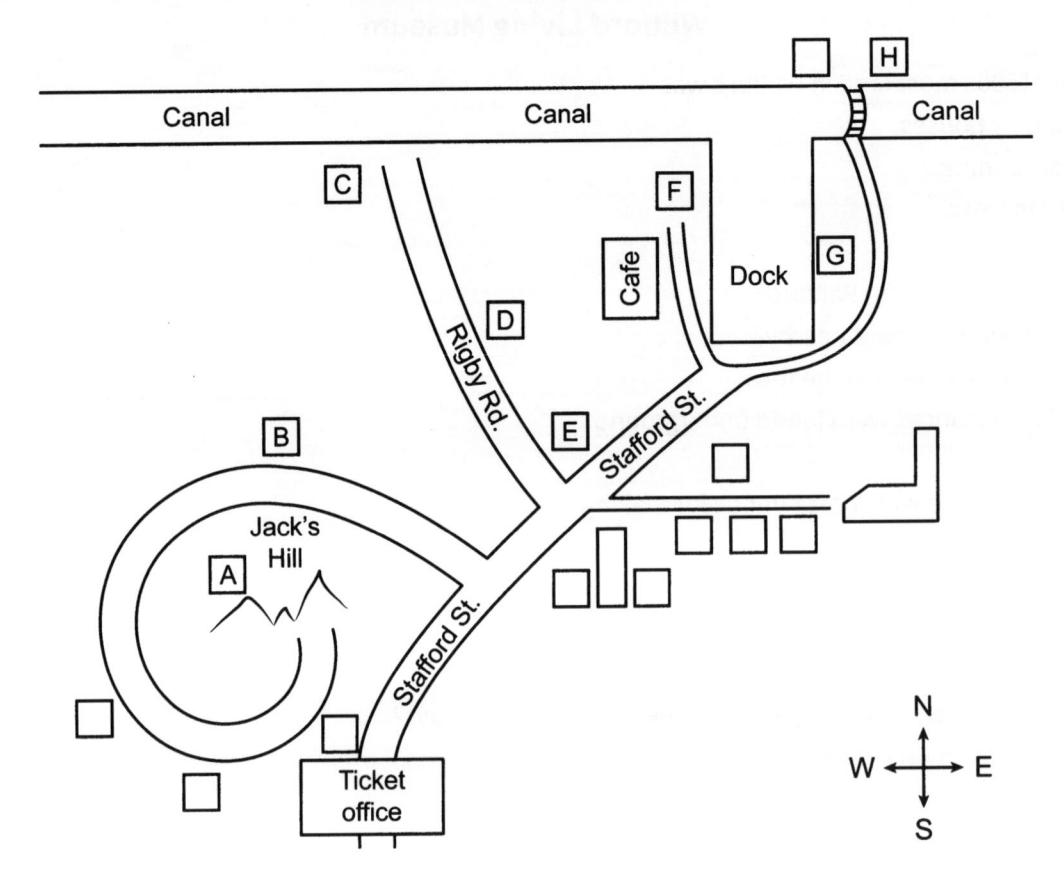

16 Old bakery ....
17 Doctor's surgery ....
18 Cooper's Cottage ....
19 Stables ....
20 Old school ....

Exam Practice Test 6 — Listening Part 3

Questions 21–22

Choose TWO letters, A–E.

According to the students, what are the TWO most important benefits of market research?

A Selecting the best advertising
B Reducing the levels of risks
C Building confidence among employees
D Saving money in the long run
E Identifying new opportunities

Questions 23–24

Choose TWO letters, A–E.

Which do the students agree are TWO valid criticisms of market research?

A It does not reveal any new information.
B Its benefits are hard to measure.
C It takes too much time to carry out.
D It makes use of too much specialist language.
E Its findings are sometimes wrong.

Questions 25–26

Choose TWO letters, A–E.

The students are surprised by the success of which TWO sources of information.

A face-to-face communication
B official government statistics
C the media and social media
D online surveys of public opinion
E filming customers as they shop

Questions 27–30

Complete the flow-chart below.

Choose **FOUR** answers from the box and write the correct letter, **A–F**, next to **Questions 27–30**.

> A written records
> B online studies
> C specific questions
> D individual responsibility
> E proper planning
> F regular meetings

Market Research Using a Business's Own Resources

Begin with staff education to maximise the chances of success.

⬇

Give staff examples of **27** .... that will be helpful every day.

⬇

The BQR Group says that staff should make use of **28** .... each week.

⬇

Having **29** .... is motivating for staff, according to *Business Guide*.

⬇

Provide detailed feedback about any changes that you decide to make.

⬇

Allow staff to have **30** .... to ensure continued participation.

Exam Practice Test 6 — Listening Part 4

Questions 31–37

Complete the notes below.

Write ONE WORD ONLY for each answer.

Drinking Water

Introduction
- Drinking water is essential for human life.
- The '8 glasses a day' rule is a myth, except for the **31** ....

Some effects of water on the body
- Drinking before **32** .... may assist weight loss.
- Dr Amaldi's study shows that water speeds up **33** ....
- A US research study showed that dehydrated bodies cannot control **34** .... so well.
- There is no evidence that drinking water results in better **35** ....

The brain
- Women who drank lots of water had fewer **36** ....
- Men suffered more **37** .... with insufficient water.

Questions 38–40

Complete the summary below.

Write ONE WORD ONLY for each answer.

Too much water?

Drinking too much water is not a common problem. Australian research has shown that people have difficulty **38** .... when they have drunk enough. But occasionally people have become sick from too much water, particularly groups of **39** .... This may be because they have high levels of **40** .... in their blood. The best advice is to drink when you are thirsty.

Earth's lakes are under threat

Lake Poopó used to be Bolivia's second largest lake. Situated in the Altiplano Mountains at an altitude of around 3,700m, the lake in winter would cover an area of some 2,700 square kilometres as it was fed by swollen rivers. With very little rainfall during summer, this reduced to around 1,000, still a remarkable size. This was the pattern in previous centuries, but in December 2015, satellites confirmed the reports of local people that the lake had gone. While scientists had suspected that Poopó would eventually run dry, they didn't expect that this would occur for at least another thousand years. The local mining industry had already contributed to the pollution of the lake, but scientists believe global warming, drought and irrigation projects are all responsible for its disappearance. Today the consequences of Lake Poopó's disappearance are dramatic; many people who lived in the villages around it have left, since there are no more fish to be caught. Environmentalists also point to the fact that the lake had been the stopover point for thousands of birds as they migrated to other regions. Their numbers will certainly fall now the lake has gone.

Lake Poopó is not the only vast area of water to have disappeared. The Aral Sea in Central Asia was once the world's fourth largest lake but then it began to shrink in the 1960s. As a shallow lake, it depended on rivers to keep its level up. But then water from these rivers was diverted for irrigation purposes. Rice is a crop that needs huge quantities of water to survive in desert areas. Fields planted with cotton also require a regular supply. Now the water level is so low that fishing has stopped altogether. And it is not just the immediate area that is affected. Because the floor of the lake is now exposed, the salt that lies there is often carried by the wind across a radius of 300 kilometres. This impacts on agriculture as it damages growing plants and is absorbed by the soil.

For some lakes, the biggest threat is from climate change. On average, the surface water of the world's lakes has gone up in temperature by 0.34°C every ten years since 1985. Lake Tanganyika in East Africa is a lake where this trend has been observed, although it is by no means the most extreme example. This would be Lake Fracksjön in Sweden, where an increase of 1.35°C per decade has been observed – a figure which is estimated to rise. For Lake Tanganyika, however, the consequences have been severe. Warming has disrupted its ecosystem, and fish numbers have dropped sharply. In turn, this decline in fish stocks has impacted on families living in villages and towns around the lake, since they have no other source of protein. Furthermore, around 100,000 people depend on the fisheries established around Lake Tanganyika. These companies provide them with regular employment, without which communities will not survive.

In Iran, Lake Urmia's waters have also been affected by unusually hot summers, but dams and irrigation projects have also played a part. In the past, people admired its beautiful green-blue colour. However, the water now has a red tint. The reason for this is that bacteria quickly multiply in the warm waters of a shallow lake. Now local communities are understandably concerned about the future. One of their concerns is that Lake Urmia is no longer seen as a place where people can bathe to improve their health. As a result, in the last decade, there has been a downturn in tourism in the area, an industry many people depended on.

In some cases, it can be a challenge for scientists to predict outcomes for a lake or to recognise the factors that threaten it. Take, for example, Lake Waiau in Hawaii, a lake that was used in healing rituals by native Hawaiians. It is a fairly small lake, approximately 100m across, with some variation as the water level rises and falls. However, in early 2010, the lake began to decrease in size. By September 2013, it could only be described as a pond. The cause of the lake's decline has not yet been established, but drought is among the suspects. Then there is Scott Lake in central Florida. In June 2006 a massive sinkhole opened up beneath the lake – acting like a plug hole in a bath. It only took two weeks for the water to drain away. Local residents called meetings to decide what action to take, but in the end, nature took care of the problem. Clay, sand and other fine material plugged the hole and the lake started to fill with water again. Nevertheless, as geologists point out, sinkholes can occur with some frequency in Florida, so there is a chance that Scott Lake will drain away again.

Questions 1-8

Complete the notes below.

*Choose **ONE WORD AND / OR A NUMBER** from the passage for each answer.*

Disappearing and Damaged Lakes

- Lake Poopó

    It covered about **1** _____ square kilometres in the dry season.

    It can no longer support people, fish or visiting **2** _____

- The Aral Sea

    It has shrunk because water is used for crops such as **3** _____ and rice.

    4 _____ from the bottom of the lake affects an area of 300 kilometres.

- Lake Tanganyika

    Families need to eat fish for its **5** _____

    Fisheries give **6** _____ to over 100,000 people.

- Lake Urmia

    The colour has changed because **7** _____ are increasing.

    8 _____ has declined in the last ten years.

Questions 9-13

Do the following statements agree with the information given in Reading Passage 1?

In boxes 9-13 on your answer sheet, write

TRUE	*if the statement agrees with the information*
FALSE	*if the statement contradicts the information*
NOT GIVEN	*if there is no information on this*

9 Scientists are surprised that Lake Poopó has disappeared so quickly.
10 Steps are being taken to reduce the impact of mining on Lake Poopó.
11 Lake Fracksjön is the fastest warming lake in the world.
12 Researchers are certain about the reason for Lake Waiau's disappearance.
13 Lake Scott's rising water level has occurred as a result of rainfall.

Biofuels: are they the fuels of the future?

Many plants can be turned into biofuels – but which ones should we use and what methods are best?

A

On paper, biofuels seem the ideal replacement for oil, coal and gas, the fossil fuels we depend upon, and which drive global warming and disrupt weather patterns by releasing carbon dioxide into the atmosphere. But the past decade has seen the biofuel industry face tough questions over whether it can truly claim to be 'green'. One of the biggest criticisms of biofuel crops – at least those that produce the fuel ethanol – has been their impact on food markets and on traditional land use. Direct impacts – for example, cutting down forests to make way for a biofuel crop – are usually obvious, says Professor Bill Laurance, director of the Centre for Tropical Environmental and Sustainability Science at James Cook University. But, in his experience, indirect impacts can be no less devastating for the environment and are far more of a challenge to anticipate.

B

Let's take Brazil, for example. When farmers in the US opted out of soy in favour of corn as a biofuel crop, soy prices soared, suddenly making it an attractive crop for Brazilian farmers. In turn, this increased demand for freshly deforested cropland in Brazil. Similar situations are occurring all over the world. But while deforestation can certainly lead to economic benefits for farmers, it also puts biodiversity at risk. Then, once a biofuel crop has been planted on deforested land, farmers need to ensure that it grows as well as it can. That means applying large quantities of fertiliser, and while this helps the plants to shoot up, there is also the possibility it will lead to the contamination of local rivers.

C

Not all biofuels have been grown on land, but the once-popular idea of generating them from microscopic algae grown in ponds or tanks has largely been forgotten. Professor Rachel Burton, leader of the ARC Centre of Excellence for Plant Cell Walls at the University of Adelaide, thinks that there is a smarter way forward for biofuels and it starts with selecting the right crop for land not usually used for agriculture. Burton and others are looking to tough plants that grow on land too dry or salty for conventional crops. Australia, for example, could turn to crops such as agave, hemp or the native saltbush and wild-growing sorghum for the biofuels of the future, she says.

D

Researchers must also consider economic factors, however. While plant oils can be extracted and turned into biodiesel for vehicles and machinery, currently the process is very expensive – much more so than the process for fossil fuels. Dr Allan Green is innovation leader for bio-based products at CSIRO Agriculture and Food. His solution is to make plants oilier by genetically altering them so that they produce oil in their leaves, not just in their fruit or seeds. With more oil being produced on a particular section of land by the same number of plants, it would become cheaper to harvest and extract the oil. The technology, which has so far only been tested in tobacco, shows that oil production can be boosted to a third or more of a tobacco leaf's weight. If used in a different crop – one that already produces oil in its seeds or fruit – the hope is that oil output could be doubled, though that idea is yet to be put to the test.

E

A technology which is becoming increasingly popular in the biofuel industry is hydrothermal liquefaction. This is a process which uses heat and pressure to break apart molecules in whole plants and remove oxygen, so that the raw material is turned into 'bio-crude oil'. Then, just as we need to refine the crude oil made from fossil fuels, the plant-based oil is also refined. After this, it can then be turned into different kinds of fuel. One advantage of the hydrothermal liquefaction process is that many kinds of plant can be used. And if this process could run on energy from solar panels or wind farms, it would be much more environmentally sustainable.

F

New processing technologies are giving biofuel producers hope that, in future, they won't be limited to plants designed to be biofuel-only crops. Perhaps they will be able to choose species that deliver added benefits or sources of income. Hemp crops, for instance, could be used for their oil, but also for their fibre. Some car manufacturers have already used it as a soundproofing material in their vehicles, and others may do the same. And according to Kirsten Heimann, associate professor at the College of Science and Engineering at James Cook University, it might be possible, say, for algae not just to act as a biofuel, but to decontaminate water. Burton believes this kind of multi-purpose use for biofuel crops is the way forward. 'It's much more sophisticated thinking,' she says. 'Biofuels maybe don't need to be as cheap as we think they do, because you can make money out of the other things.' Eventually, the biofuel industry could well develop into a very diverse one, with no one crop or process dominating the market, according to Green. 'The amount of fuel we need to move away from petroleum is massive, so there's plenty of space for all technologies,' he says.

Questions 14-19

Reading Passage 2 has six paragraphs, **A-F**.

Which paragraph contains the following information?

14 a theory about oil production which must still be proved
15 an overview of the stages in a particular biofuel manufacturing method
16 examples of the uses that biofuel crops might have apart from providing energy
17 an explanation of the way that fossil fuel use harms the environment
18 reference to a particular biofuel production method being abandoned
19 a comparison between the production costs for biofuels and for other kinds of fuel

Questions 20-23

Look at the following statements (Questions 20-23) and the list of researchers below.

Match each statement with the correct researcher, **A**, **B** or **C**.

NB You may use any letter more than once.

20 It would be more cost-effective if a biofuel was used for a range of products.
21 It is not always easy to predict what effects the use of biofuels crops may have.
22 A variety of biofuel crops and manufacturing processes will be required in future.
23 It would be best to use biofuel crops that can survive in difficult environmental conditions.

List of researchers
A Professor Bill Laurance
B Professor Rachel Burton
C Dr Allan Green

Questions 24-26

Complete the sentences below.

Choose **ONE WORD ONLY** from the passage for each answer.

24 The decision by US farmers to grow .... had an effect on land in Brazil.
25 .... is threatened when trees are cut down so crops can be planted.
26 Rivers may be polluted by the .... that farmers use on biofuel crops.

Exam Practice Test 6 — Reading Passage 3

*You should spend about 20 minutes on **Questions 27–40**, which are based on Reading Passage 3 below.*

Team Building
If you thought ancient monuments were built in honour of gods and kings, think again, says Laura Spinney

At Poverty Point in the US state of Louisiana, a remarkable monument overlooks the Mississippi river. Built around 3,500 years ago entirely from earth, it consists of six semi-circular ridges and five mounds. 'Mound A', as archaeologists refer to it, is the largest at 22 metres high. The earth mounds at Poverty Point are not just impressive, they are also intriguing. Ancient monuments have always been regarded as products of large, hierarchical societies, built as tributes to gods and kings. But the creators of the Poverty Point monument were hunter-gatherers, who functioned in a more democratic way. They may have looked to elders for guidance, but these would not have exerted a commanding influence over their small groups. So who, or what, motivated building on such a grand scale?

Archaeologists have been excavating Poverty Point for more than a century. However, the truly remarkable nature of Mound A only emerged a few years ago. This was when a team led by Tristram Kidder of Washington University drilled into the mound. They saw for the first time that it consisted of neat layers of differently coloured earth. It rains a lot around Poverty Point, and we know that fluctuations in temperature and increased flooding eventually led to its abandonment. But Kidder could see no sign that the layers had combined, as you might expect if it had rained during construction. Kidder reached a startling conclusion: Mound A must have been built in one short period, perhaps in as little as 30 days, and probably no more than 90.

Mound A contains nearly 240,000 cubic metres of earth; the equivalent of 32,000 truckloads. There were no trucks then, of course, nor any other heavy machinery, animals like mules to carry the earth, or wheelbarrows. Assuming it did take 90 days, Kidder's group calculated that around 3,000 basket-carrying individuals would have been needed to get the job done. Given that people probably travelled in family groups, as many as 9,000 people may have assembled at Poverty Point during construction. 'If that's true, it was an extraordinarily large gathering,' says Kidder. Why would they have chosen to do this?

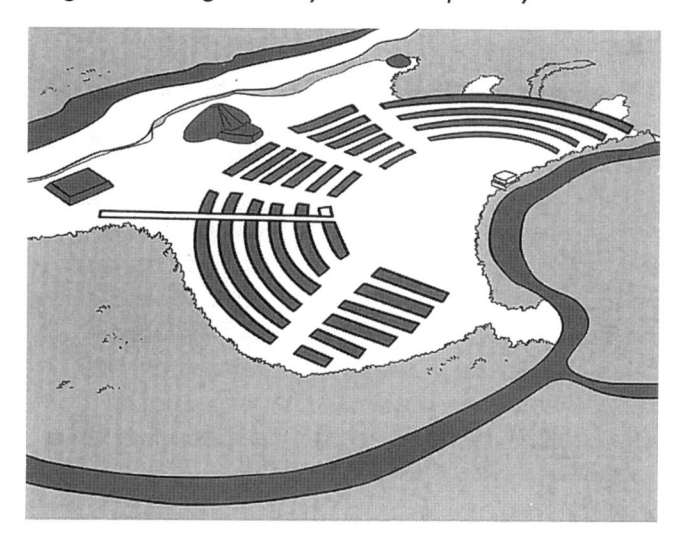

Another archaeologist, Carl Lipo, thinks he has the answer: the same reason that the people of Easter Island built their famous stone heads. When Lipo first when to Easter Island, the prevailing idea was that the enormous statues had been rolled into place using logs, and the resulting deforestation contributed to the human population's collapse. But Lipo and fellow archaeologist Terry Hunt showed the statues could have been 'walked' upright into place by cooperating bands of people using ropes, with no need for trees. They argue further that by making statues, people's energy was directed into peaceful interactions and information-sharing. They ceased crafting statues, Lipo claims, precisely because daily existence became less of a challenge, and it was no longer so important that they work together.

An ancient temple known as Göbekli Tepe in south-east Turkey is another site where a giant team-building project might have taken place. Since excavations started, archaeologists have uncovered nine enclosures formed of massive stone pillars. Given the vast size of these pillars, a considerable workforce would have been needed to move them.

But what archaeologists have also discovered is that every so often, the workers filled in the enclosures with broken rock and built new ones. The apparent disposability of these monuments makes sense if the main aim was building a team rather than a lasting structure. Indeed, the many bones from animals such as gazelle found in the filled-in enclosures suggest people held feasts to celebrate the end of a collaborative effort.

A number of researchers share Lipo's view that the need to cooperate is what drove monument makers. But as you might expect when a major shift in thinking is proposed, not everyone goes along with it. The sceptics include Tristram Kidder. For him, the interesting question is not 'Did cooperative building promote group survival' but 'What did the builders *think* they were doing?' All human behaviour comes down to a pursuit of food and self-preservation, he says. As for why people came to Poverty Point, he and his colleagues have suggested it was a pilgrimage site.

If Lipo is right, have we in any way inherited our ancestors' tendency to work together for the sake of social harmony? Evolutionary biologist David Sloan Wilson thinks we have. Wilson cites the Burning Man festival, promoted as an experiment in community and art, which draws thousands of people to Nevada's Black Rock Desert each summer. Among the ten principles laid down by co-founder Larry Harvey are 'inclusion' and 'communal effort'. Another is 'leaving no trace', meaning that whatever festival-goers create they destroy before departing. In this way, the desert landscape is only temporarily disturbed. Wilson says there is evidence that such cooperative ventures matter more today than ever because we are dependent on a wider range of people than our ancestors were. Food, education, security: all are provided by people beyond our family group. Recently, as part of his Neighbourhood Project in Binghamton, Wilson and his colleagues helped locals create their own parks. 'This brought people together and enabled them to cooperate in numerous other contexts,' he explains. This included helping with repairs after a series of floods in 2011. Social psychologist Susan Fiske of Princeton University also sees value in community projects. Her research shows, for example, that they can help break down the ill-informed views that people hold towards others they have observed but do not usually interact with. So if modern projects really help build better communities, that will surely be a monumental achievement.

Questions 27–32

Do the following statements agree with the claims of the writer in Reading Passage 3?

In boxes 27–32 on your answer sheet, write

- **YES** if the statement agrees with the claims of the writer
- **NO** if the statement contradicts the claims of the writer
- **NOT GIVEN** if it is impossible to say what the writer thinks about this

27 The whole monument at Poverty Point was made out of earth.
28 The monument at Poverty Point was the first of its kind to be built in the US.
29 The older members of the tribes at Poverty Point had great power over their people.
30 It is surprising that archaeologists took so long to discover the existence of Mound A.
31 Tristram Kidder's work at Mound A revealed something previously unknown to researchers.
32 A change in weather patterns forced people living around the Poverty Point monument to move away.

Questions 33–36

*Choose the correct letter, **A**, **B**, **C** or **D**.*

Write the correct letter in boxes 33–36 on your answer sheet.

33 The writer refers to trucks, mules and wheelbarrows in order to
   A highlight the technical ability of the Poverty Point inhabitants.
   B emphasise the number of workers required to build the mound.
   C question the logic of choosing Poverty Point as a place for construction.
   D challenge the idea that the mound could have been made so quickly.

34 Archaeologist Carl Lipo's research at Easter Island has led him to believe that
   A people had to cut down trees in order to transport larger statues.
   B remote communities faced greater environmental challenges than other societies.
   C islanders stopped making statues when their lives became easier.
   D methods of making the statues varied amongst different groups.

35 According to the writer, excavations at Göbekli Tepe suggest that
   A there was disagreement between groups over the temple's design.
   B human occupation drove certain animal populations into decline.
   C each of the enclosures that were built served a different purpose.
   D the builders had no intention of creating permanent structures.

36 In the sixth paragraph, what are we told about Tristram Kidder?
   A He feels the academic community should support Carl Lipo's theory.
   B He has changed his mind about the purpose of the Poverty Point monument.
   C He doubts that Carl Lipo has identified the key reason for monument making.
   D He believes that most people recognise the need to help each other to survive.

Questions 37–40

*Complete the summary using the list of words, **A–I**, below.*

*Write the correct letter, **A–I**, in boxes 37–40 on your answer sheet.*

| A basic needs | B different generations | C new infrastructure | D human activities |
| E negative impressions | F emergency situations | G commercial advertising | H economic growth |

Examples of cooperation in modern times

David Wilson believes that events such as the Burning Man festival encourage social harmony. For example, participants in the festival cooperate so **37** .... won't permanently affect the desert environment. In Wilson's opinion, cooperation is especially important today because we now rely on many people for our **38** .... Wilson also points to how community projects such as park creation can lead to improved group efforts in **39** .... Psychologist Susan Fiske has also shown how **40** .... can change when community projects encourage interaction between strangers.

Exam Practice Test 6 — Writing Tasks 1–2

Writing Task 1

You should spend 20 minutes on this task.

The diagram below shows how honey is made in small-scale commercial production.

Summarise the information by selecting and reporting the main features, and make comparisons where relevant.

Write at least 150 words.

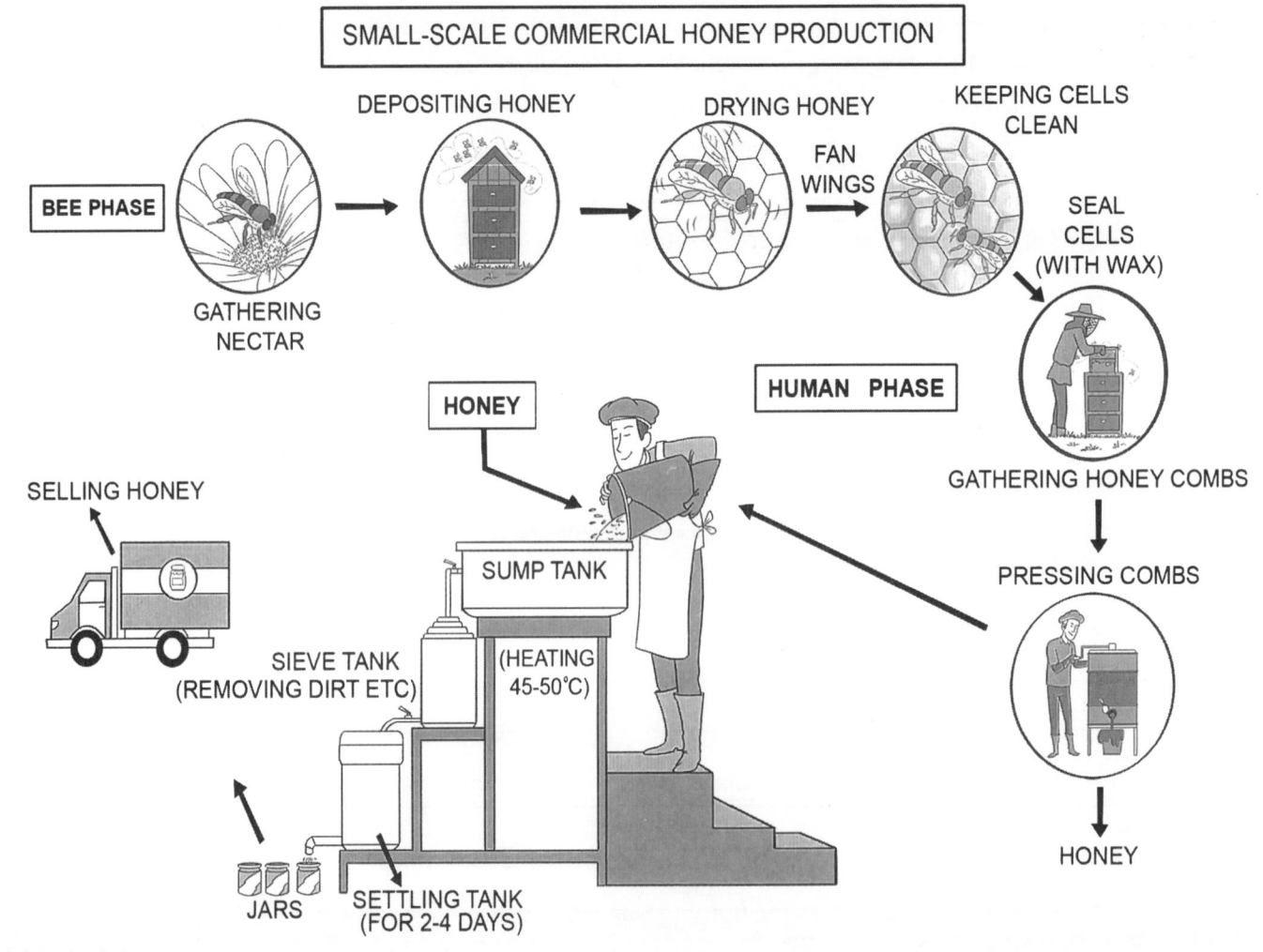

SMALL-SCALE COMMERCIAL HONEY PRODUCTION

BEE PHASE
- GATHERING NECTAR
- DEPOSITING HONEY
- DRYING HONEY (FAN WINGS)
- KEEPING CELLS CLEAN
- SEAL CELLS (WITH WAX)

HUMAN PHASE
- GATHERING HONEY COMBS
- PRESSING COMBS
- HONEY
- SUMP TANK (HEATING 45-50°C)
- SIEVE TANK (REMOVING DIRT ETC)
- SETTLING TANK (FOR 2-4 DAYS)
- JARS
- SELLING HONEY

Writing Task 2

You should spend 40 minutes on this task.

Write on the following topic:

In many parts of the world, children and teenagers are spending more and more of their time indoors.

What do you think are the causes of this problem?

What measures could best be taken to solve it?

Give reasons for your answer and include any relevant examples from your own knowledge and experience.

Write at least 250 words.

Exam Practice Test 6 — Speaking Parts 1-3

Speaking Part 1

The examiner will start by introducing him/herself and checking your identity. He or she will then ask you some questions about yourself and then go on to ask you some questions about one or two other topics, for example:

Let's talk about cars.
- Do you like travelling by car?
- Is the colour of a car important to you?
- Do you prefer to drive or to be a passenger in a car?
- What kind of car would you like to have in the future?

or

Let's talk about primary / elementary school.
- What was the best thing about your primary / elementary school?
- Which subject did you not like at your primary / elementary school?
- Are you still in touch with some of your friends from primary / elementary school?
- In the future, would you like to send a child of yours to the same primary / elementary school?

Speaking Part 2

The examiner will give you a topic like the one below and some paper and a pencil.
The examiner will say:

I'm going to give you a topic and I'd like you to talk about it for one to two minutes. Before you talk, you'll have one minute to think about what you're going to say. You can make some notes if you wish. [1 minute]

All right? Remember you have one to two minutes for this, so don't worry if I stop you. I'll tell you when the time is up. Can you start speaking now, please?

> **Describe a song that you will always remember.**
>
> **You should say:**
> what the song is
> when and where you first heard this song
> what you liked about this song
>
> **and explain why you will always remember this song.**

The examiner may ask one or two rounding-off questions when you have finished your talk, for example:
- Do your friends like this song too?
- Do you listen to a lot of songs?

Speaking Part 3

The examiner will ask some general questions which are connected to the topic in Part 2. You will usually have to answer up to six questions.
The examiner will say, for example:

We've been talking about a song that you will always remember. I'd like to discuss with you one or two more general questions relating to this. First, let's consider listening to music.
- What types of music do young people in your country enjoy listening to?
- What is different about listening to music at home and going to a live concert?

Let's talk about music in everyday life.
- Why do so many people listen to music when they are travelling to work/college?

Finally, let's talk about the future of music.
- Should governments subsidise less popular forms of music such as opera? Why do you think that?

Sample Answer Sheet for Listening

IELTS Listening Answer Sheet

Candidate Name:
Candidate No.:
Centre No.:
Test Date: Day / Month / Year

Listening Listening Listening Listening Listening Listening Listening

#	Answer	#	Answer
1		21	
2		22	
3		23	
4		24	
5		25	
6		26	
7		27	
8		28	
9		29	
10		30	
11		31	
12		32	
13		33	
14		34	
15		35	
16		36	
17		37	
18		38	
19		39	
20		40	

Marker 2 Signature:
Marker 1 Signature:
Listening Total:

REPRODUCED WITH THE PERMISSION OF CAMBRIDGE ASSESSMENT ENGLISH
© UCLES 2019

Photocopiable

Sample Answer Sheet for Reading

IELTS Reading Answer Sheet

Candidate Name:

Candidate No.: 　　　　　Centre No.:

Test Module: ☐ Academic　☐ General Training　Test Date: Day __ Month __ Year ____

Reading		Reading	
1		21	
2		22	
3		23	
4		24	
5		25	
6		26	
7		27	
8		28	
9		29	
10		30	
11		31	
12		32	
13		33	
14		34	
15		35	
16		36	
17		37	
18		38	
19		39	
20		40	

Marker 2 Signature:　　Marker 1 Signature:　　Reading Total:

61788

REPRODUCED WITH THE PERMISSION OF CAMBRIDGE ASSESSMENT ENGLISH
© UCLES 2019

Photocopiable

Sample Answer Sheet for Writing

BRITISH COUNCIL   **idp**   **Cambridge Assessment English**

IELTS Writing Answer Sheet - TASK 1

Candidate Name

Candidate No.　　Centre No.

Test Module ☐ Academic ☐ General Training　　Test Date　Day　Month　Year

If you need more space to write your answer, use an additional sheet and write in the space provided to indicate how many sheets you are using:　Sheet ☐ of ☐

Writing Task 1　Writing Task 1　Writing Task 1　Writing Task 1

Do not write below this line

Do not write in this area. Please continue your answer on the other side of this sheet.

REPRODUCED WITH THE PERMISSION OF CAMBRIDGE ASSESSMENT ENGLISH
© UCLES 2019

Photocopiable

Sample Answer Sheet for Writing

IELTS Writing Answer Sheet - TASK 2

Candidate Name:
Candidate No.:
Centre No.:
Test Module: ☐ Academic ☐ General Training
Test Date: Day / Month / Year

If you need more space to write your answer, use an additional sheet and write in the space provided to indicate how many sheets you are using: Sheet ___ of ___

Writing Task 2   Writing Task 2   Writing Task 2   Writing Task 2

Do not write below this line

Do not write in this area. Please continue your answer on the other side of this sheet.

REPRODUCED WITH THE PERMISSION OF CAMBRIDGE ASSESSMENT ENGLISH
© UCLES 2019

Photocopiable

Acknowledgements

Our highly experienced team of Trainer writers, in collaboration with Cambridge English Language Assessment reviewers, have worked together to bring you *IELTS Trainer 2 Academic*.

We would like to thank Anthea Bazin (writer), Amanda French (writer), Miles Hordern (writer), Katy Salisbury (writer), Carole Allsop (reviewer), Michael Black (reviewer), Anthony Cosgrove (reviewer) and Heather Daldry (reviewer) for their work on the material.

The authors and publishers acknowledge the following sources of copyright material and are grateful for the permissions granted. While every effort has been made, it has not always been possible to identify the sources of all the material used, or to trace all copyright holders. If any omissions are brought to our notice, we will be happy to include the appropriate acknowledgements on reprinting and in the next update to the digital edition, as applicable.

Text

Key: LP = Listening Part, RP = Reading Passage, T = Test.

T2 RP2: The Guardian for the adapted text from "Sleep should be prescribed': what those late nights out could be costing you' by Rachel Cooke, *The Guardian*, 24.09.2017. Copyright © 2017 The Guardian. Reproduced with permission; T6 RP2: The Guardian for the adapted text from 'Biofuels: could agave, hemp and saltbush be the fuels of the future?' by Dyani Lewis, *The Guardian*, 10.05.2017. Copyright © 2017 The Guardian. Reproduced with permission; T6 RP3: New Scientist Ltd. adapted text from the article 'Team Building' by Laura Spinney, *New Scientist Ltd.*, 10.01.2018, Copyright © 2018 New Scientist Ltd. All rights reserved. Distributed by Tribune Content Agency. Reproduced with permission.

Photography

All photographs are sourced from Getty Images.

T2 LP4: Stephen Spraggon/Photo Library T4 RP3: MarioGuti/E+.

Illustration

QBS Learning.

Audio

Audio recordings by DN & AE Strauss Ltd. Engineer: Neil Rogers; Editor: James Miller; Producer; Dan Strauss. Recorded at Cambridge Assessment, Cambridge.